SELECTED POEMS

James Schuyler

SELECTED POEMS

Farrar · Straus · Giroux

NEW YORK

Farrar, Straus and Giroux
19 Union Square West, New York 10003

Library of Congress Control Number: 2007921511
ISBN-13: 978-0-374-53089-1
ISBN-10: 0-374-53089-0

www.fsgbooks.com

1   3   5   7   9   10   8   6   4   2

For Daniel Newman

Contents

vii

ix

Introduction

by John Ashbery

Everything chuckles and creaks
sighs in satisfaction
reddens and ripens in tough gusts of coolness
and the sun smites

These are the closing lines of a poem by James Schuyler whose title is
"Today." Unlike most of his poems, it is dated—July 26, 1965—which
means that he wrote it while staying with the Fairfield Porter family at
their summer home on Great Spruce Head Island off the coast of
Maine. The poem begins: "The bay today breaks / in ripples of ap-
plause," and proceeds to tabulate the sights and sounds of an unre-
markable but pleasant day in the open air. The list itself, we are given
to understand, is a sufficient reason for its own existence. ("What is, is
by its nature, on display," a line from an early villanelle called "Poem,"
could stand as Schuyler's aesthetic credo.)

Above all, no judgments are passed. The bay's applause is its own
business: it likes what it sees, apparently, or it may be applauding it-
self. It is part of the "everything" that chuckles, creaks, sighs, reddens,
and ripens. These acts are seen not as contradictory: chuckles and
creaks coexist happily, as do reddening and ripening, which aren't al-
ways identical. A sigh is just a sigh. Everything is noted, and accepted
for what it is, and not in Margaret Fuller's sense of "I accept the uni-
verse." Schuyler's acceptance seeks no credit, asks no acknowledg-
ment. It just is, like Today itself. But then the sun "smites"—an
alarming coda to a hitherto docile catalog of maritime country mat-
ters. *Et in Arcadia ego* . . .

As a person, Schuyler was not unlike his poems. Quiet (sometimes
disconcertingly so), kind, wickedly observant, often content to live his

life in spaces created by others and to celebrate their lives, families, landscapes, interiors, and pets, and very occasionally exploding into rage that he usually kept carefully suppressed. Born on November 9, 1923, in Chicago, to Marcus Schuyler and his wife Daisy, he grew up first in the Washington suburb of Chevy Chase. "City, begone / From my thoughts," he writes, addressing "whited Washington" in "Hymn to Life." "Childhood was not all that gay. Nor all that gray, / For the matter of that."

On the whole, though, his happiest years were probably the earliest ones, before the parents separated and eventually, in 1929, divorced. Schuyler would later describe his father, a journalist with *The Washington Post*, as "an enchantingly wonderful man, a heavy, jolly, well-read man," words that could apply to the son as well. In 1931 his mother married a building contractor named Fredric Ridenour, and the family, soon to be augmented by another son, moved to East Aurora, New York, a town made famous by the pop philosopher Elbert Hubbard and his Roycroft school of arts and crafts. And James Schuyler reluctantly became James Ridenour. In his autobiographical poem "A Few Days," he says, "Ridenour was my stepfather's name, and when I went to / Europe in 1947 I found my name had never legally been changed . . . / It's good to / have your own name." Indeed, there was little love between Schuyler and his stepfather, who once confiscated the son's library card apparently out of sheer meanness. Schuyler would later compare home life to "a novel by Dostoevsky."

After briefly attending Bethany College in West Virginia, Schuyler enlisted in the navy in 1943 and saw combat in the North Atlantic. At a trial during which his homosexuality was mentioned, he was discharged after going AWOL in New York. A small family inheritance allowed him to travel to Europe in 1947 with his boyfriend, Bill Aalto. They bicycled through France and visited W. H. Auden and his companion Chester Kallman, friends from New York, at their house on the Italian island of Ischia; for a time Schuyler worked as Auden's secretary and typed the manuscript of his collection *Nones*. Until then, he had entertained notions of becoming a writer, but working on the Auden manuscript caused him to reflect, "If this is poetry, I'm certainly never going to write any myself."

Not until he was back in New York did Schuyler seriously begin writing, at the relatively late age of twenty-six. His early, fascinating experiments in poetry and prose were eventually collected in the 1971 volume *The Home Book*. As far as I can recall, the earliest poems date from around 1951, when he met other aspiring young writers such as Frank O'Hara, Kenneth Koch, Barbara Guest, and myself. (Eventually we would become known as the New York School of Poets, a term coined by the art dealer John Bernard Myers, though nobody told us about that at the time.)

One of his earliest poems, "Salute," appeared in *The New Yorker*; it stands as the portal to this volume of *Selected Poems*, and became a kind of emblem of his poetry, for him and for us all. Like "Today," it is an inventory of things found in nature; despite the New York label, Schuyler was always happiest in the country. Its transparent language and wry Epicurean outlook would remain constants throughout his career. "Past is past," he begins; no use crying over spilled milk. Long ago he had wanted to collect one of each kind of "clover, / daisy, paintbrush" (the flower names, taught to him by his grandmother, are heart-catchingly Schuylerian, and of course his mother's name was Daisy) "that grew in that field / the cabin stood in" (otherwise unidentified), so as to "study them one afternoon / before they wilted." He never got around to it, of course. Besides, would it really have been worth doing? Not "if one / remembers what one meant / to do and never did," since "is not to have thought to do / enough?" It is, at least it is in Schuyler's comforting world-view, which accepts failure as a higher kind of success. Read this way, the incidents of his disappointing life—chronic poverty, bouts of mental illness, and a vicarious existence as a houseguest for years on end—point toward happiness. To have thought to do is, sub specie aeternitatis, enough. The road to heaven is paved with good intentions.

Though he was seldom able to hold a job for long, he had a gift for being taken care of—first by his lovers Charles Heilemann and Arthur Gold, later by the Porter family, and in his last years by a consortium of friends who helped pay his bills and his room at New York's Hotel Chelsea. This had its positive side. Except for periods of debilitating depression, he was mostly free to write when and how he chose, to "loafe" and invite his soul. In fact, he does sometimes strike a Whitmanesque note, albeit one swiftly countered with a wisecrack, as when he writes in "Hymn to Life": "May leans in my window, offering hornets. / To them too I give leave to go about their business, which is not / Nesting in my books." (A few lines later it's Dickinson's turn: "May / Opens wide her bluest eye and speaks in bird tongues and a / Chain saw.") This beautiful poem—one of a sequence of long-lined, long-limbed quasi-epic poems that includes "A Few Days," "The Crystal Lithium," and "The Morning of the Poem"—can easily stand comparison with those of his two nineteenth-century precursors: it is a high point in our poetry, dazzling in its lyric grandeur and its American plainness. The endless, swaying lines, like surf on a calm day, are Schuyler's invention. They tell little more than how March half-heartedly morphs into April, which in turn becomes the lovely and puzzling month of May: "May mutters, 'Why / ask questions?' or, 'What are the questions you wish to ask?'" Caught in the lines' loose meshes, however, are recollections, philosophical questions, remembered snatches of conversation (rarely attributed), notes on the light and shadows or the rain: "The rain comes back, this spring, like a thirsty dog / Who goes back and back to his dish. 'fill it up, please,' wag wag." Like all his poetry, it is an *invitation au voyage* to the pleasures of loafing, the opposite of laziness. Random reading, letters to and from friends, long naps (he once told me how he missed an appointment because he'd grabbed forty winks—"at one minute per wink"), observing cars and birds outside the window—these, he gives us to understand, are really what life is made of.

Frank O'Hara once said that after listening to Haydn's music for long periods of time, he felt he wanted to hear nothing else (this from a passionate fan of the uncompromising art of Cage and Feldman), and after immersing myself in Schuyler's music I often feel it's all I need—all other poetry is somehow present there. Though he is in a sense saying the same thing again and again, it is, like the pages of one's diary, always new. The poems are seldom "about" anything in the way poetry traditionally is; they are the anything. To reread him is to live, as though life were an experience one had just forgotten and been newly awakened to: "A story not told: so much not understood, a sight, an insight . . ." There is no space between the story, always the same, and the way of telling, which is as invisible and vital as the air.

It produces a pleasure unlike any other, one of the most unalloyed I know of.

JOHN ASHBERY's latest collection is *A Worldly Country*. *Notes from the Air: Selected Later Poems* will be published in 2007 by Ecco/HarperCollins. He is Charles P. Stevenson Jr. Professor of Languages and Literature at Bard College.

FROM

Freely Espousing

[1 9 6 9]

Salute

Past is past, and if one
remembers what one meant
to do and never did, is
not to have thought to do
enough? Like that gather-
ing of one of each I
planned, to gather one
of each kind of clover,
daisy, paintbrush that
grew in that field
the cabin stood in and
study them one afternoon
before they wilted. Past
is past. I salute
that <u>various</u> field.

Past , present , Future

3

Freely Espousing

a commingling sky

        a semi-tropic night
        that cast the blackest shadow
        of the easily torn, untrembling banana leaf

or Quebec! what a horrible city
so Steubenville is better?
            the sinking sensation
when someone drowns thinking, "This can't be happening to me!"
the profit of excavating the battlefield where Hannibal whomped the
    Romans
the sinuous beauty of words like allergy
the tonic resonance of
pill when used as in
"she is a pill"
on the other hand I am not going to espouse any short stories in
    which lawn mowers clack.
No, it is absolutely forbidden
for words to echo the act described; or try to. Except very directly
as in
bong. And tickle. Oh it is inescapable kiss.
Marriages of the atmosphere
are worth celebrating
            where Tudor City
catches the sky or the glass side
of a building lit up at night in fog
"What is that gold-green tetrahedron down the river?"
"You are experiencing a new sensation."

      if the touch-me-nots
      are not in bloom
      neither are the chrysanthemums

the bales of pink cotton candy
in the slanting light
> are ornamental cherry trees.
> The greens around them, and
> the browns, the grays, are the park.

It's. Hmm. No.
> Their scallop shell of quiet
> is the S.S. *United States*.
> It is not so quiet and they
> are a medium-size couple who
> when they fold each other up
> well, thrill. That's their story.

February

A chimney, breathing a little smoke.
The sun, I can't see
making a bit of pink
I can't quite see in the blue.
The pink of five tulips
at five P.M. on the day before March first.
The green of the tulip stems and leaves
like something I can't remember,
finding a jack-in-the-pulpit
a long time ago and far away.
Why it was December then
and the sun was on the sea
by the temples we'd gone to see.
One green wave moved in the violet sea
like the UN building on big evenings,
green and wet
while the sky turns violet.
A few almond trees
had a few flowers, like a few snowflakes
out of the blue looking pink in the light.
A gray hush
in which the boxy trucks roll up Second Avenue
into the sky. They're just
going over the hill.
The green leaves of the tulips on my desk
like grass light on flesh,
and a green-copper steeple
and streaks of cloud beginning to glow.
I can't get over
how it all works in together
like a woman who just came to her window
and stands there filling it
jogging her baby in her arms.
She's so far off. Is it the light

that makes the baby pink?
I can see the little fists
and the rocking-horse motion of her breasts.
It's getting grayer and gold and chilly.
Two dog-size lions face each other
at the corners of a roof.
It's the yellow dust inside the tulips.
It's the shape of a tulip.
It's the water in the drinking glass the tulips are in.
It's a day like any other.

A Reunion

Week after week glided away in the St. Clare mansion . . .
HARRIET BEECHER STOWE

You will like their upstairs
papered with wrappers off Blue Goose oranges.
You will like their grandmother.
They keep up her grave.
You may get to like them.

"The Elizabethans Called It Dying"

Beyond Nagel's Funeral Parlor
      ("Your cousin says you filled her station wagon up;
        I didn't say it your cousin said it")
and (is it a perpetual wake they have
or just a popular parlor?)
        the novelty ice cream cake and soda shop
        the boys hang out in front of
        until they're eighteen then move across the street
in front of the saloon   Munich beer on draught
not forgetting the big church with the doleful bells
cheerily summoning housewives to early Mass
        ("The good thing about religion is
          it gives a man a sense of his place in the universe")
to Carl Schurz Park
kept reasonably free of la-di-da
after all the Mayor lives in it
in the huge glare of the electric sign on Doctors' Hospital
that says HOSPITAL
what are they trying to do, solicit trade in Queens?
or is that Welfare Island?
the river races upstream, neap tide turned
past the posh apartments
        did you ever sit back and try to remember
        whether particular paving stones were hex- or octagons?
        seen once at night and presumably memorized
          sloshing around in the rain
your eyes lips and nostrils
vary a distinct and unique shape—
        why it's The Raindrop Prelude!
home—
        not to be in love with you
I can't remember what it was like
        it must've been lousy

Fabergé

"I keep my diamond necklace in a pond of sparkling water for invisibility.

"My rubies in Algae Pond are like an alligator's adenoids.

"My opals—the evening cloud slipped in my pocket and I felt it and vice versa.

"Out of all the cabs I didn't take (a bit of a saver) I paved a street with gold. It was quite a short street, sort of a dollhouse cul-de-sac.

"And there are a lot of other pretties I could tell about—ivory horses carved inside bone dice; coral monkeys too tiny to touch; a piece of jade so big you might mistake it for the tundra and a length of chalcedony as long as the Alcan Highway which is the Alcan Highway. It is solidified liquid chalcedony.

"Here, just for you, is a rose made out of a real rose and the dewdrop nestled in a rosy petal that has the delicate five-o'clock-shadow fuzz—blue—is not a tear. I have nothing to cry about now I have you."

A White City

My thoughts turn south
a white city
we will wake in one another's arms.
I wake
and hear the steampipe knock
like a metal heart
and find it has snowed.

December

Il va neiger dans quelques jours

FRANCIS JAMMES

The giant Norway spruce from Podunk, its lower branches bound,
this morning was reared into place at Rockefeller Center.
I thought I saw a cold blue dusty light sough in its boughs
the way other years the wind thrashing at the giant ornaments
recalled other years and Christmas trees more homey.
Each December! I always think I hate "the overcommercialized
        event"
and then bells ring, or tiny light bulbs wink above the entrance
to Bonwit Teller or Katherine going on five wants to look at all
the empty sample gift-wrapped boxes up Fifth Avenue in swank
        shops
and how can I help falling in love? A calm secret exultation
of the spirit that tastes like Sealtest eggnog, made from milk solids,
vanillin, artificial rum flavoring; a milky impulse to kiss and be
        friends.
It's like what George and I were talking about, the East-West
Coast divide: Californians need to do a thing to enjoy it.
A smile in the street may be loads! you don't have to undress
        everybody.
                    "You didn't *visit* the Alps?"
                    "No, but I saw from the train they were black
                    and streaked with snow."
Having and giving but also catching glimpses
hints that are revelations: to have been so happy is a promise
and if it isn't kept that doesn't matter. It may snow
falling softly on lashes of eyes you love and a cold cheek
grow warm next to your own in hushed dark familial December.

A Man in Blue

Under the French horns of a November afternoon
a man in blue is raking leaves
with a wide wooden rake (whose teeth are pegs
or rather, dowels). Next door
boys play soccer: "You got to start
over!" sort of. A round attic window
in a radiant gray house waits like a kettledrum.
"You got to start . . ." The Brahmsian day
lapses from waltz to march. The grass,
rough-cropped as Bruno Walter's hair,
is stretched, strewn and humped beneath a sycamore
wide and high as an idea of heaven
in which Brahms turns his face like a bearded thumb
and says, "There is something I must tell you!"
to Bruno Walter. "In the first movement
of my Second, think of it as a family
planning where to go next summer
in terms of other summers. A material ecstasy,
subdued, recollective." Bruno Walter
in a funny jacket with a turned-up collar
says, "Let me sing it for you."
He waves his hands and through the vocalese-shaped spaces
of naked elms he draws a copper beech
ignited with a few late leaves. He bluely glazes
a rhododendron "a sea of leaves" against gold grass.
There is a snapping from the brightwork
of parked and rolling cars.
There almost has to be a heaven! so there could be
a place for Bruno Walter
who never needed the cry of a baton.
Immortality—
in a small, dusty, rather gritty, somewhat scratchy
Magnavox from which a forte
drops like a used Brillo pad?

Frayed. But it's hard to think of the sky as a thick glass floor
with thick-soled Viennese boots tromping about on it.
It's a whole lot harder thinking of Brahms
in something soft, white and flowing.
"Life," he cries (here, in the last movement),
"is something more than beer and skittles!"
"And the something more
is a whole lot better than beer and skittles,"
says Bruno Walter,
darkly, under the sod. I don't suppose it seems so dark
to a root. Who are these men in evening coats?
What are these thumps?
Where is Brahms?
And Bruno Walter?
Ensconced in resonant plump easy chairs
covered with scuffed brown leather
in a pungent autumn that blends leaf smoke
(sycamore, tobacco, other),
their nobility wound in a finale
like this calico cat
asleep, curled up in a breadbasket,
on a sideboard where the sun falls.

Sestina

A translation of Dante's *Al poco giorno* . . .

I have reached, alas, the long shadow
and short day of whitening hills
when color is lost in the grass.
My longing, all the same, keeps green
it is so hooked in the hard stone
that speaks and hears like a woman.

In that same way this new woman
stands as cold as snow in shadow,
less touched than if she had been stone
by the sweet time that warms the hills
and brings them back from white to green,
dressing them in flowers and grass.

Who, when she wreathes her hair with grass,
thinks of any other woman?
The golden waves so mix with green
that Love himself seeks its shadow
that has me fixed between small hills
more strongly than cemented stone.

More potent than a precious stone,
her beauty wounds, and healing grass
cannot help; across plains and hills
I fled this radiant woman.
From her light I found no shadow
of mountain, wall, or living green.

I have seen her pass, dressed in green,
and thought the sight would make a stone
love, as I, even her shadow.
And I have walked with her on grass,

speaking like a lovesick woman,
enclosed within the highest hills.

But streams will flow back to their hills
before this branch, sappy and green,
catches fire (as does a woman)
from me, who would bed down on stone
and gladly for his food crop grass
just to see her gown cast shadow.

The heavy shadow cast by hills
this woman's light can change to green,
as one might hide a stone in grass.

An Almanac

Shops take down their awnings;
women go south;
few streetlamp leaners;
children run with leaves running at their backs.
In cedar chests sheers and seersuckers displace flannels
                                        and wools.

Sere leaves of the Scotch marigolds;
crystals of earth melt;
the thorn apple shows its thorns;
a dog tracks the kitchen porch;
wino-hobos attempt surrender to warm asylums.

Caged mink claw;
gulls become pigeons;
snow bends the snow fence.
Heavy food;
rumbling snowplows.

Seats in the examination hall are staggered.
The stars gleam like ice;
a fragment of bone;
in the woods matted leaves;
a yellowish shoot.
A lost key is found;
storm windows are stacked on the beams of the garage.

Hudson Ferry

April what an ice-cold promise
I saw a cherry almost in bloom today
one of five magnolias opened all its buds
wide and pointing at the sun
going down in front of City Hall

they cleaned it. It looks new.
Why can't they stop cleaning things
and sweep the streets. Like the April weather
you can't talk about the weather
it's like saying my lady's damask cheek

look at the smoke blazing over Jersey
the flats are on fire it's like a flushed cheek
and nearer a smokestack blows a dense dark blue
smoke is hot it looks cold trailing like hair
the bite-me kind springy or flung about

you can't get at a sunset naming colors
the depth the change the charge deep out of deep
the flaring upward what it nails on houses
the smoke swiftly pouring at the stack
hangs lazy wide and scarce dispersed

look at Esta, Isador and Alvin bright
rosy-gilded with wind-burnished cheeks
laughing and chatting in the wind
above the slap and river hoots
and there's Miss Strong Arm, toting her torch

it's another city going back
the moon one night past its full
writes signs vanishing hypnotically

downtown the towers block massively
at the rail a man who rests his hands

looks heroic: he works at night: going from or to?
I don't know I hardly know why I'm on the river
late at night. It's a bore, waiting for a train
reading a tabloid. The City Hall all clean
gleams like silver like the magnolias in the moonlight

April and Its Forsythia

It's snowing on the unpedimented lions. On ventilator hoods
white triangles. It evens up wrinkled tar roofs,
smooths out rough concrete coping, showing the shape
of a wall—between coping top and roof. The census
taker was just here. She had on transparent overshoes, coat and
hat: are clothes less secret? Less snowlike?
Snow isn't secret, showing further aspects, how small
cast lions would look if they grew maned, tame yet whitely
fierce; how the center of the sidewalk is always a path
steps tend to, as across a plain, through a wood; how cars
swing out heavily and big at a corner, turning voluminously
as a fleshy dancer. That census taker. I'm the head of a household.
I am also my household. Not bad. It's still snowing, down
and across: when cloth gets old and stretched, a twill
may have a gusty, snowy movement. Rough on poor rats
who work in it, must go out in it: it's dirty cold wet slush
underfoot, you hear it under wheels: swoosh, and slop
when they stop. Mr Merzag, the super, loves it. Used to drop
to 30 below the nine months he spent in Siberia. There
they really get snow! Not just wet feathers, like New York.
What variety snow falls with and has: this kind lays like wet sheets
or soaked opaque blotting paper: where a surface makes
a natural puddle, its own melting darkens it, as though it had lain
all winter and the thaw is come. Is this change in weather in early
      April
just what the sugarbush needed, upstate and further up, New
      Hampshire, Vermont?
Maple syrup production is off, the *Times* says, due to the vogue for
      maple furniture.
Willingly or not, you can't give your Cape Cod cobbler's table
with a lamp attachment above a ship's-type wheel back to its grove.
Now it falls on two diagonals, except it's more: the depth dimension
of air. Ugh. The head of this household is going out in it.
Willingly or not, I'll check up on Central Park
where branches of sunshine were in bloom on Monday.

Roof Garden

tubs of . . .
        memory
for a moment
     won't supply a name
          not portulacas
                (". . . she had on her
                new dressmaker dress and
                spectator pumps . . .")
petunias
     tubs of pink petunias
a gray roof
     black when it's hot
light grays today
          green tubs of punctured glow
             before a glowing wall
all the walls reflecting light
at six on a summer evening
            the petunias shimmer in a breeze
a long, long time ago
          petunias
adorable, sticky flower

May 24th or so

Among white lilac trusses, green-gold spaces of sunlit grass.
The shade side of a clothes pole, dark innards of a light-violet shell.
Everything trembles
everything shakes
in the great sifter:
bud scales, pollen, all the Maytime trash
whose sprinkles are clocks that tell
the time of the dandelion take-over generation,
never quite coming to pass.
A man passes
in calendula-colored socks.
A robin passes

        zip

          thud

punctuating the typescript of today with a comma on the too-close
    cut grass.
Then erases it for a full stop in a lilac.
In Y's and V's and W's
an elm ascends
smoothly as an Otis Elevator.
Other trade-marks blur in the gone-over forsythia hedge.
A table and a chair, carved chunkily in the lawn,
are the colors of an oystershell as though beneath the sod were
    chalk not sand.
Why it seems awfully far
from the green hell of August
and the winter rictus,
dashed off, like the easiest thing

Today

July 26th, 1965

The bay today breaks
in ripples of applause.
The wind whistles.
Spruce and bright-leaved birch
at the edge
are flat yet plump
as letters with "see enclosures."
A gull mews, the mailboat toots,
the wind rises and pours with a noise like water
and spills black jazz
from spiked brown seed cups of red columbine.
The wind takes with it
a wrack of voices: "the who?"
and unintelligible shapes of phrases
or one scrape: hickory on cement.
Across the bay today
a white house smaller than a thumbnail moon
shines like the light
it shows at night, a star
or sun of kerosene.
The barn swallows from the eaves
are up to something, maybe
showing their fledglings how to do it, scything
an insect harvest from the air.
Round and brown as rabbit droppings,
seed pods of blue-eyed grass
bobble and split along the seams:
so big for so small a flower.
A sailboat scuds,
a poplar tugs at roots
in soil a scurf on rock.

23

Everything chuckles and creaks
sighs in satisfaction
reddens and ripens in tough gusts of coolness
and the sun smites

Sorting, wrapping, packing, stuffing

dirty socks in dirty sneakers
capless tubes of unguents among brushes and septic Band-Aids
adhesive flowers into spongy books
when the great bronze bell
sounds its great bronze bong
it will find a lifetime jar of Yuban Instant in my right hand,
in my left, Coleman's Mustard.
But how do you pack a blue fire escape—even if the man
got off it out of the 97 degree sun
and blizzards, then sullied snow that left
disclosing no car where one was. Excuse me, druggist,
can you take this blue fire escape out of my eye?
       (no, no one is going to ask anyone to take anything
       out of a heart, not even a tear with a hambone in it.
       All there is
       is blood and thump.)

Now the blue fire escape
is packed, and it is
already tomorrow O little brown bat guano
of course it is still today
with the bay crinkling at the edges
of a tomorrow when Creeping Charlie and Stinking Willie flourish
                    under glass on the moon.
Imagine going to the sun for the winter
if it's like Miami
Or getting an earth burn
Or

better we should slip into this Ice Age remnant granite boulder
and grab a snooze
it is too much like packing
on Saturn

where they have poison ivy like we have Himalayas
poisonous only to planets

                              give us a gingham smile
red white and checkered
Help
              the blue fire escape!
it's coming unpacked all over the floor like a Milky Way
lighting the north
an aurora borealis of neckties

                                        Knize
                                        Sulka
                                        Au Chardon d'Ecosse

stuff wrap cram snap
              "Hello Lincoln?
              I want to store
              a blue fire escape."

How pretty, rising from the long Memorial Pool
among toy boats all day and stars all night
glittering and cold as Santa Claus
                              "See you at The Petunia Pump.
                              More later."

The time is getting out of hand
                        splash splash
cut down the books
to fit an Oshkosh nutshell
                        My Heart Is Like a Green Canoe
                        The World Is a Long Engagement Party
                        The Great Divorce Has Been Annulled
                        Romance of Serge Eisenstein
                        Immanuel Kant, Boy Detective
                        Emma Kant, Mother of Men
                        Judy Kant, R.N.
The spruce have stopped shrinking
they never began and great hunks of the world will fit

26

Seeking

for old New England
in old trials: to each conviction
what percentile of unapprehended
drunks, lustful lookers, sleights-of-finger?
Unless the convicted
were innocent as witches. There is that
about old New England.
People understand each other better than that
usually, though, no matter how they testify
guardedly on the phone: "It's not just
that she's lazy, has round heels and sews
Paris labels in Klein's clothes:"
as the bird feigning lameness
draws to itself yet more to the nest the attention it seeks to thwart.
Here is its nest, in this old New England
woodpile: three robin's-egg-blue
robin's eggs: ergo: that lame bird was a big healthy robin
though it dropped dead at your feet. That's
just DDT. The romance
of certain old clothes
may be merely olfactory. Still, there must've been a lot of
watched pots under stovepipe hats
("Seen Walcott's new 'Pilgrim' beaver?")
and a stranger from Spain
found the freedom to kiss
and play kissing games a
little hard to take. Later,
liked it. Real old New Englanders: viz. Juanita
Walcott y Gomez, Blue Juanita
corrupted to *Blue Juniata*. That was later, and farther west
where the wild rice lightly rattled into canoes
and the better people came from the East
humming, "By the Rude Bridge"
and, "Flower from the Caerulean Wall." You can't get far enough

from old New England (humming, "The Lowell Factory Girl
    Song")
since you can't get any nearer.
This hair bracelet won't tell us much
(a late, Hispano-Dutch, connection: somewhere along the line
the Juanita link pops up
in Gomez Walcott y van Aau)
nor this portrait of old Judge Lindsey Wooley
"The scourge of the Passamaquody,"
a collateral of Blue Juanita's. Say, who are these bug-big
old New Englanders pursuing and pursued by
red men the height of a red mite? The sun is white
on clapboards in green Wiscasset
and in a cellar hole
dusky tulips
incline their heads.
                              "*Maine* isn't old New England!"
Maine is Maine I can hardly remember
when it was still Massachusetts
or where Emma Eames lived (Bath)
or the birthplace of Maxine Elliott (Rockland)
or Edna St. Vincent Millay or her island (Matinicus)
or Robert Tristram Coffin humming "Forever Is Not Far"
                (wonder where he fits in the
"Judge and Mrs. Wooley v. A. Tristram-Gomez take pleasure"
    picture?)
You remember, her daughter by hubby no. 1, Lindsey Coffin:
    Frani
the girl with the labels. She married a bohunk from Scranton:
Mlokosewitsch.
(Paeonia Mlokosewitschii!
large globular
perfect complement
jade-green of leaves and pink petioles
of unusual distinction
                        indeed. Mlokosewitsch
                            you live on

honored in old New England
                                        like *Epilobium angustifolium*
Great Rose Willow Herb or common fireweed
                in early August
                                                summoning fall
Remember to slam the parentheses behind you
) bang and) bang and)) double bang
(to be on the safe side).
Here are seven lucky stones
                        OOOOOOo
found in old New England. And a snail shell @
                        the common Nash
                        the stately Reo
dumped in old New England bays
                        metal reefs
                        instant housing
for fishy prey of predator fish.
"Conservation," says the bulletin of Our Lady of the Sea,
"is true charity." The wood church looking out
over wrinkle-rocked Stonington
its doors wide open to all the thanksgivers who can't crowd in
for the contract the Crotch Island Quarry got
for the granite to build the Memorial
after a year-long layoff. Old New Englanders
(with names like Haskell and Cacciacavallo)
eating an island out of the sea
like the wonderful fish and terrible food
at Glad's Lunch

Milk

Milk used to come in tall glass, heavy and uncrystalline as frozen melted snow. It rose direct and thick as horse-chestnut tree trunks that do not spread out upon the ground even a little: a shaft of white drink narrowing at the cream and rounded off in a thick-lipped grin. Empty and unrinsed, a diluted milk ghost entrapped and dulled light and vision.

Then things got a little worse: squared, high-shouldered and rounded off in the wrong places, a milk replica of a handmade Danish wooden milk bat. But that was only the beginning. Things got worse than that.

Milk came in waxed paper that swelled and spilled and oozed flat pieces of milk. It had a little lid that didn't close properly or resisted when pulled so that when it did give way milk jumped out.

Things are getting better now. Milk is bigger—half a gallon, at least—in thin milky plastic with a handle, a jug founded on an oblong. Pick it up and the milk moves, rising enthusiastically in the neck as it shifts its center of weight. Heavy as a breast, but lighter, shaping itself without much changing shape: like bringing home the milk in a bandana, a neckerchief or a scarf, strong as canvas water wings whose strength was only felt dragged under water.

On the highway this morning at the go-round, about where you leave New Hampshire, there had been an accident. Milk was sloshed on the gray-blue-black so much like a sheet of early winter ice you drove over it slowly, no matter what the temperature of the weather that eddied in through the shatterproof glass gills. There were milk-skins all around, the way dessert plates look after everyone has left the table in the Concord grape season. Only bigger, unpigmented though pretty opaque, not squashed but no less empty.

Trembling, milk is coming into its own.

Going

In the month when the Kamchatka bugbane
finally turns its strung-out hard pellets white
and a sudden drench flattens the fugitive
meadow saffron to tissue-paper scraps
and winds follow that crack and bend without breaking
the woody stems of chrysanthemums so the good of not disbudding
shows in lower smaller flights of metallic pungency,
a clear zenith looks lightly dusted and fades to nothing
at the skyline, shadows float up to lighted surfaces
as though they and only they kept on the leaves
that hide their color in a glassy shine.
A garnering squirrel makes a frantic chatter at a posse of cats
that sit and stare while their coats thicken. Days
are shorter, more limpid, are like a kiss
neither dry nor wet nor on the lips
that sends a light shock in rings
through all the surface of the skin. Early, in the middle
of the afternoon, the light slants
into rooms that face southwest: into this room
across a bookcase so the dead-brown gold-stamped
spines look to be those to take down now:
Hodge and His Masters, The Cereals in America.
If a leaf of gold were beaten to transparency,
and all that here roots and extrudes were tarnished silver
and blackened bronze—bumped and brushed against
here and there into highlights—
were seen through it by the wind-flickered quick-setting sun,
October would look no different than it looks

The Master of the Golden Glow

An irregular rattle (shutters) and
a ferule tapped
on a blackboard—or where you come from
do they say chalkboard?—anyway it's not any sort of pointer
it's a sash facing west
wood and glass drummed on by autumn tatters.
Say, who are you
anyway? "I think we may have met before.
God knows I've heard enough about you."
That largest maple—
half its leaves an undreamt-of butter:
if only safflower oil
were the color of its name
the way olive oil is. "Why,
don't you *like* butter?"
The doctor's youngest son
paddles the canoe while he (the doctor) casts
for mud-flavored carp in the long brackish pond:
Agawam, meaning lake. Lake Pond,
Pond Lake, Lake Lake, Pond Pond,
its short waves jumping up and down
in one place with surplus energy to spend.
Somewhere, out of the wind,
the wind collects a ripe debris.
"I'll tell you who I am: someone
you never met
though on a train you studied a boil on my neck
or bumped into me
leaving a late late party
                    'Sorry'
or saw throwing bones in the ocean
for an inexhaustible retriever."
The wind drops. The sky darkens
to an unfathomable gray

and through hardware cloth one
leaf is seen to fall
describing the helixes of conch-shell cores
gathered in summer, thrown out in autumn.
More litter, less clutter.

Stun

If you've ever been in a car
that was hit by a train
whang
(a tearing like metal shears)
flip   spin
              "Why I'm perfectly OK!"
this streaming blood
a euphoric sweat of thanksgiving
and later

a hunk of scrap iron
just there on the turnpike
for no reason
flies up and
whang
it goes on your new underneath
well, it's like you were thrown
grabbed by the scruff of the neck —
head over heels right into Proust's steamy cup
just another crumb
of scalloped cookie
odious and total memory
                        (of the cells, no doubt)
in prickle-green, speed-lashed
Massachusetts

Proust = poet
memeory circulation in your mind

34

Poem

How about an oak leaf
if you had to be a leaf?
Suppose you had your life to live over
knowing what you know?
Suppose you had plenty money

"Get away from me you little fool."

Evening of a day in early March,
you are like the smell of drains
in a restaurant where pâté maison
is a slab of cold meat loaf
damp and woolly. You lack charm.

35

Now and then

For Kenward Elmslie

up from the valley
now and then a chain saw rising to a shriek, subsiding to a buzz
"Someone" is "cutting in his wood lot" another day
shows they are not
someone is two men clearing shoulders
of a narrow high-crowned road
stacked poles were lately saplings
the leaves on the slash gone limp, unstarched, unsized
one man with one fierce eye and where the other should be
an ill-knit cicatrix
men who don't make much aren't much
for spending what they do
on glass eyes, tooth-straightening devices ("a mouth
like the back of a switchboard"), nose jobs, dewenning operations
a country look prevails
and a vestigial fear of the evil eye lurks
". . . my skin creeps . . ."
                      Out of Adamant Co-op
men in "overhauls" step into evening rising
in long-shadowed bluish haze to gold and pink
by Sodom Lake (was it that any Bible name
was an OK name?) and boys stare unabashed
and unaggressive not what the man on the bus fled
from his one-day job talking excitedly about
"teen-age Puerto Rican tail-bait" and
"You can *have* New York!" Some present
you'd rather have wouldn't you an apple tree
that climbed up into keels over
sad, and too bad, the best apples on Apple Hill
still, it can be propped or budded on new stock or just
that it once was there
                  Driving past, driving down, driving over
along the Winooski

through the home of Granite City Real Ice Cream
The Monument Capitol
buildings of rusticated granite marred
to our eyes by etched polished granite remodeled downstairs
may be found by a future happily heterodox
"There's a touch of autumn—
                                there's another touch of autumn"
and the dark tranquility of hemlocks encroaching on untilled fields
"You can't make a living
plowing stones" subsistence
farming is well out of style: "You can't call it living
without the margin"
coveted obsolescence!
a margin like that on this page
a paper luxury "Collectors"
the lady in the antique shop said "are snapping up
silver" "Since we're off the silver standard?" "Why,
maybe so" Perhaps
six 1827 Salem coin-silver spoons for $18
or what about
"Have you *The Pearl of Orr's Island?*"
"That's a book I'd want to read myself.
I'm from here but live in Florida.
Winters are too hard: 40 below.
You don't feel it though
like zero in Boston. I'll take St. Johnsbury any day
over Boston."
                    Over St. Johnsbury the clouds shift in curds
and a street goes steeply down
into Frenchtown by the railroad station
into which anachronistically comes
a real train: yesterday's torment of dust-exhaling plush
on the backs of bare knees today's nostalgia
but not much. Curls cut out of wood, brick
of a certain cut and color, a hopped-up cripple
on a hill above his pond, a slattern
frowning at the early-closed state liquor store,

an attic window like a wink,
The Scale Co., St. Johnsbury has everything
        Not this high hill a road
going in undergrowth leads up to
by walls of flat cleared-field stones
so many and so long a time to take
so much labor so long ago and so soon
to be going back, a host to hardhack
and blueberry baby steps
first fallings from a sky
in which the wind is moving furniture
the upholstery of summer coming all unstitched
the air full of flying kapok
and resolutions: "remember to fetch the ax
whack back pine intrusions"
from the road turning down to a lower field
and across the roughest one the County keeps
a woman and a boy come up
on heavy horses. "Morning!
Had frost
last night at Adamant.
Might have a killing frost
tonight." Quick and clear as the water
where cress grows the cold
breaks on the hills to the soft crash
of a waterfall beyond
a beaver pond
and slides on
flinging imaginary fragments of cat's ice
from its edges to flash
a bright reality in the night sky and it—
the cold—stands, a rising pool, about
Sloven's farmhouse and he dreams
of dynamite. A bog sucks
at his foundations. Somewhere a deer
breaks branches. The trees
say *Wesson. Mazola*

replies a frog.

It doesn't happen though the cold
that is not that night. It happens all right
not then when the white baneberry
leans secretively where a road forks
met with surprise: "Why here it is:
the most beautiful thing." The spirit
of Gelett Burgess sets Mother Nature
gabbing. *"That's* my *Actea pachypoda*, dear, we
call it Doll's-Eyes." Got up as smart
as ever in muck and dank she belches
—" 'Scuse: just a touch of gas"—
swamp maple flames and ambles over and plunks
down on a dead rubber tire
to contemplate smashed glass and a rusty tin
and "Some of my choicer bits: that
I call Doctor's Dentures. These
are Little Smellies." Not
the sort you look to meet so near
gold-domed, out-of-scale Montpelier
a large-windowed kind of empty public bigness
so little to show, so much
to take pride in rather more than on the way to Stowe
a pyrocrafted maple board in a Gyp-o-teria
IF MORE MEN WERE SELF STARTERS
FEWER WIVES WOULD HAVE TO CRANK.
Welcome to the chair lift and cement chalet.

Days
of unambiguous morning when dawn
peels back like a petal to disclose blue depths
deep beyond all comprehending and tall field growth bends
with a crushing weight of water cut
into sac-shaped portions, each less than a carat
and which streak an early walker's trouser legs
"You're soaked!" crossing on a door
the spill to where nodding ladies' tresses
pallidly braid their fragrance and the woods

emit their hum. Days
when the pond holds on its steel one cloud
in which thin drowned trees stand:
spare shapes of winter when summer
is just loosening to fall and bits of ribbon
from an electric typewriter patch a screen.
Croquet days, scissors-and-paste nights
after dinner on the better sort of ham
and coffee strong enough to float a goose egg.
Are those geese, that V, flying so early?
Can it be so late? in the green state
needles, leaves, fronds, blades, lichens and moss create
                    Can it be so soon before the long white
refrozen in frost on frost
on all twigs again will flash
cross cutting star streaks—the atoms
dance—on a treacherous night
in headlights?

                    "Horrible Cold Night
Remain at Home"

                    "Clear and Beautiful
Remain at Home"

40

Buried at Springs

There is a hornet in the room
and one of us will have to go
out the window into the late
August mid-afternoon sun. I
won. There is a certain challenge
in being humane to hornets
but not much. A launch draws
two lines of wake behind it
on the bay like a delta
with a melted base. Sandy
billows, or so they look,
of feathery ripe heads of grass,
an acid-yellow kind of
goldenrod glowing or glowering
in shade. Rocks with rags
of shadow, washed dust clouts
that will never bleach.
It is not like this at all.
The rapid running of the
lapping water a hollow knock
of someone shipping oars:
it's eleven years since
Frank sat at this desk and
saw and heard it all
the incessant water the
immutable crickets only
not the same: new needles
on the spruce, new seaweed
on the low-tide rocks
other grass and other water
even the great gold lichen
on a granite boulder
even the boulder quite
literally is not the same

II

A day subtle and suppressed
in mounds of juniper enfolding
scratchy pockets of shadow
while bigness—rocks, trees, a stump—
stand shadowless in an overcast
of ripe grass. There is nothing
but shade, like the boggy depths
of a stand of spruce, its resonance
just the thin scream
of mosquitoes ascending.
Boats are light lumps on the bay
stretching past erased islands
to ocean and the terrible tumble
and London ("rain persisting")
and Paris ("changing to rain").
Delicate day, setting the bright
of a young spruce against the cold
of an old one hung with unripe cones
each exuding at its tip
gum, pungent, clear as a tear,
a day tarnished and fractured
as the quartz in the rocks
of a dulled and distant point,
a day like a gull passing
with a slow flapping of wings
in a kind of lope, without
breeze enough to shake loose
the last of the fireweed flowers,
a faintly clammy day, like wet silk
stained by one dead branch
the harsh russet of dried blood.

FROM

The Home Book:
Prose and Poems
1951-1970

[1 9 7 7]

Poem

I do not always understand what you say.
Once, when you said, across, you meant along.
What is, is by its nature, on display.

Words' meanings count, aside from what they weigh:
poetry, like music, is not just song.
I do not always understand what you say.

You would hate, when with me, to meet by day
What at night you met and did not think wrong.
What is, is by its nature, on display.

I sense a heaviness in your light play,
a wish to stand out, admired, from the throng.
I do not always understand what you say.

I am as shy as you. Try as we may,
only by practice will our talks prolong.
What is, is by its nature, on display.

We talk together in a common way.
Art, like death, is brief; life and friendship long.
I do not always understand what you say.
What is, is by its nature, on display.

Jelly Jelly

Summer apples, showy and sugary, mealy and touchy
a finger bruise on the thin skin
brown and silently reproachful as your wife's black eye.

But if September apples ripen
and the sun coats the sights with crinkling sheets
of cold while the waves come yapping
something about "wine dark"
evening primroses in clefts of rocks they lap
in a space labeled, "August 27th, 1965
pay on demand," why then it is
September
when pebbles turn, shedding a summer snow
of salt, palely glowing in the first fall beaches.

The wind is pendant-breasted as a naked Swede.
A frosted fox grape shows
where a bird shat as it ate.
Blackberry canes arch and obtrude big nipples.
And the chaste tree blooms.

Back before I made the egg test
I thought the world as flat and very like an elderberry umbel
full of round juicy people winking and waving,
crying "Hi!" and "Meet you in the jelly!"
or "Under the lid of an elderberry pie."

A Head

A dead boy living among men as a man
called an angel
by me, for want of a word,
spaniel-eyed: wet, with bits
of gold deep in the eyeballs
hidden, like a mysterious ingredient
(*c'est là, le mystère*)
fringed with black and with black,
thick-grown, delicately thumb-smudged eyebrows
and brown cast on the face
so the lips are an earth red
and the rings or pouches under the eyes
are dark, and all the blue
there is hovers in the hollows
under the ridges of the cheekbones
as, in fall haze, earth,
broken into clods, casts shadows on itself:

except what, in the small hours, shows
the razor's path, its wide swaths
along the cheeks and down below
the strong and bluntly heart-shaped chin
where the taut flesh loosens and softens,
heaviest at the corners of the mouth
turning petulantly down from the fold
that lifts the upper lip and points
to the divider of the nostrils.

This so-called angel
who steps back into the shadows of an empty door
and staggers on short flights of stairs
is filled with a kind of death
that feeds on little things:
fulfilled plans that no longer suit the hour,

appetites that sicken and are not slaked
(such as for milk shakes),
lost or stolen handkerchiefs,
invisible contagion
(such as the common cold).

Within this head where thought repeats
itself like a loud clock, lived
the gray and green of parks before spring
and water on a sidewalk between banks of snow,
a skylit room whose windows were paintings
of windows with views of trees
converging in the park all parks imply;
in that head a million butterflies
took flight like paper streamers and bits of paper
a draught lifts at a parade.

Then they went away.
They went away in a dance-step
to the tune of "Poor Butterfly"
played on a wind-up phonograph
of red mahogany stuck with bits
of gold: right stele for him.

When night comes and lights come on
after the colors fade in the sky,
may he minister as he can to whom he may,
himself or other, give what grace
all the little deaths he stands for,
to me, have left him. He is an angel
for his beauty. So what
if it fades and dies?

FROM

The Crystal Lithium

[1 9 7 2]

Empathy and New Year

A notion like that of empathy
inspires great distrust in us,
because it connotes a further
dose of irrationalism and mysticism.
LÉVI-STRAUSS

I

Whitman took the cars
all the way from Camden
and when he got here
or rather there, said,
"Quit quoting," and took the next
back, through the Jersey meadows
which were that then. But
what if it is all, "Maya,
illusion?" I
doubt it, though. Men are not
so inventive. Or
few are. Not knowing
a name for something proves nothing. Right
now it isn't raining, snowing, sleeting, slushing,
yet it is
doing something. As a matter of fact
it is raining snow. Snow
from cold clouds
that melts as it strikes.
To look out a window is to sense
wet feet. Now to infuse
the garage with a subjective state
and can't make it seem to
even if it is a little like
What the Dentist Saw
a dark gullet with gleams and red.
"You come to me at midnight"
and say, "I can smell that after-

51

Christmas letdown coming like a hound."
And clarify, "I can smell it
just like a hound does."
So it came. It's a shame
expectations are
so often to be counted on.

New Year is nearly here
and who, knowing himself, would
endanger his desires
resolving them
in a formula? After a while
even a wish flashing by
as a thought provokes a
knock on wood so often
a little dish-like place
worn in this desk just holds
a lucky stone inherited
from an unlucky man. Nineteen-sixty-
eight: what a lovely name
to give a year. Even better
than the dogs': Wert
(". . . bird thou never . . .")
and Woofy. Personally
I am going to call
the New Year, Mutt.
Flattering it
will get you nowhere.

II

Awake at four and heard
a snowplow not rumble—
a huge beast
at its chow and wondered
is it 1968 or 1969?
for a bit. 1968 had
such a familiar sound.

52

Got coffee and started
reading Darwin: so modest,
so innocent, so pleased at
the surprise that *he*
should grow up to be *him*. How
grand to begin a new
year with a new writer
you really love. A snow
shovel scrapes: it's
twelve hours later
and the sun that came
so late is almost gone:
a few pink minutes and
yet the days get
longer. Coming from the
movies last night snow
had fallen in almost
still air and lay
on all, so all twigs
were emboldened to
make big disclosures.
It felt warm, warm
that is for cold
the way it does
when snow falls without
wind. "A snow picture," you
said, under the clung-to
elms, "worth painting." I
said, "The weather operator
said, 'Turning tomorrow
to bitter cold.'" "Then
the wind will veer round
to the north and blow
all of it down." Maybe I
thought it will get cold
some other way. You
as usual were right.

It did and has. Night
and snow and the threads of life
for once seen as they are,
in ropes like roots.

In January

After Ibn Sahl

The yard has sopped into its green-grizzled self its new year
    whiteness.

A dog stirs the noon-blue dark with a running shadow and dirt
    smells cold and doggy

As though the one thing never seen were its frozen coupling
    with the air that brings the flowers of grasses.

And a leafless beech stands wrinkled, gray and sexless—all bone
    and loosened sinew—in silver glory

And the sun falls on all one side of it in a running glance, a
    licking gaze, an eye-kiss

And ancient silver struck by gold emerges mossy, pinkly
    lichened where the sun fondles it

And starlings of anthracite march into the east with rapid jerky
    steps pecking at their shadows.

In Earliest Morning

an orange devours
the crusts of clouds and you,
getting up, put on
your daily life
grown somewhat shabby, worn
but comfortable, like old jeans: at the least,
familiar. Water
boils, coffee
scents the air
and level light plunges
among the layering boughs of a balsam fir
and enflames its trunk.
Other trees are scratched
lightly on the west.
A purposeful mutt
makes dark marks
in blue dew. The day
offers so much, holds
so little or is it
simply you who
asking too much take
too little? It is
merely morning
so always marvelously
gratuitous and undemanding,
freighted with messages
and meaning: such
as, day
is different from the night
for some; see
the south dazzle
in an effulgence
thrown out by an ocean;
a myriad iridescence

of green;
the shape
of the cold egg
you break
and with a fork
again break
and stir and pour
into a pan, where it lightly hisses.
The sediment
in your mind sinks
as something rises
in it, a thought
perhaps, like a tree when it
is just two green
crumpled bits of tape
secured to grit; a
memory—beyond
a box of Gold Dust
laundry soap a cherry
in full flower and
later full of fruit;
a face, a name
without a face,
water with a name:
Mediterranean, Cazenovia, or
iced, or
to be flushed
away; a
flash of
good humor, no
more than a
wink; and the sun
dims its light
behind a morning
Times of cloud.

An East Window on Elizabeth Street

For Bob Dash

Among the silvery, the dulled sparkling mica lights of tar roofs
lie rhizomes of wet under an iris
from a bargain nursery sky: a feeble blue with skim milk blotched
on the falls. Junky buildings, aligned by a child
("That's very good, dear") are dental:
carious, and the color of weak gums ("Rinse and spit"
and blood-stained sputum and big gritty bits
are swirled away). Across an interstice
trundle and trot trucks, cabs, cars,
station-bound fat dressy women
("I never thought I'd make it")
all foundation garments and pinched toes. I don't know how
it can look so miraculous and alive
an organic skin for the stacked cubes of air
people need, things forcing up through the thick unwilling air
obstinate and mindless as the glorious swamp flower
skunk cabbage and the tight uncurling punchboard slips
of fern fronds. Toned, like patched, wash-faded rags.
Noble and geometric, like Laurana's project for a square.
Mutable, delicate, expendable, ugly, mysterious
(seven stories of just bathroom windows)
packed: a man asleep, a woman slicing garlic thinly into oil
(what a stink, what a wonderful smell)
burgeoning with stacks, pipes, ventilators, tensile antennae—
that bristling gray bit is a part of a bridge,
that mesh hangar on a roof is to play games under.
But why should a metal ladder climb, straight
and sky-aspiring, five rungs above a stairway hood
up into nothing? Out there
a bird is building a nest out of torn-up letters
and the red cellophane off cigarette and gum packs.
The furthest-off people are tiny as fine seed
but not at all bug-like. A pinprick of blue
plainly is a child running.

Scarlet Tanager

"—in the big maple
behind the willow—"
ajet with limp spring greens
lance-like, or the head of a pike
and there it flies
and there it sits
the tanager, the bright spot
in the sunny rather evil day
the red touch green
cries out for—the soldier
in "Storm at Castelfranco."
And the drums beat
in East 95th Street
for soldiers in a storm
no, it's only a parade.
A huge and sullen Buddha
of a man waits at the starting
with his sign DOWN WITH DOVES
kids cry cadence and a bunch
of thick short men in little hats
that announce them vets
of the War to End War
(It Floats, They Laughed, Chu Chin Chow)
look defiant at those
who go counter to them
though merely strolling home.

            A couple of men jump
            out of the sky
            wearing flags. Someone
            "described as a bystander"
            gets tarred and feathered.

Embittered object of our anxious
and unworthy fears, the scapegoat

in a getup like a grackle
that a cat drags in. Glorious day
in May when by the window
a wistaria hangs its violet lights
creased with a sunny pallor
and other birds than tanagers—
fluffy balls of fluffy dung—
flit to a skirl of bagpipes
in undefoliated yards
between backs of rows of houses
and men with faces like happy fists
march in well-remembered but unpracticed step
—who would study
to forget?—or is it habit, merely,
like LOOK BEFORE YOU TURN—
waving little flags, why then why then
it's hard not to believe the marchers
march for the fun of marching
to an inward tune like Mahler's happy
happy children's song
                        drums   drums

Light Blue Above

Light blue above, darker below, lightly roughened by the stirring air
and with smooth tracks on it. There goes Reynald Hardie's lobster
boat, taking a colorful load of pleasure-seeking shoppers to Camden.

O Air

the clear, the soot-bearer, the unseen that rips
that kills and cures, that keeps
all that is empty filled, the bright invisible

into which we move like fingers into gloves
that coats our rolling home with the sweet softness
between grape and grape skin

in silent laughter in a glass pushed down
into a basin at retreating puzzled water
constrained to rise elsewhere up
the sides of the basin, of the glass
up fingers and hand and wrist

clinging to arm hair in mercurial bubbles
that detach and rise and join itself

the quick to heal
that wriggles up from hot
heat-wave pavement like teased hair
or has a wintry bite, or in the dog days saps
or is found at the bottom
of a mailbox on an empty house
or in a nest between twigs, among eggs

and we go on
with it within us
upon a dust speck
in bubble air

The Edge in the Morning

Walking to the edge with a cup of coffee
Sunup.
The sky is red.
Sunrise.
That way, the water is blinding.
That way, the water is dusted with sleep.
That way, the water shines as freshly as lead curling smoothly under
 a knife.
The bay has a skin.
It swells it without breaking like water brimming in a glass.
On its skin and on mine the sun is warm.
The slipping air is thin and cold and cools the cup.
The coffee is cold.
Small fat gray-brown birds in the grass bounce up from shadow to
 shadow.
The false oats are ripened and bearded straw.
The sun strikes them.
They light up.
The quaking grass has collapsed in wire heaps.
It is not what it was.
The edges of the bay are thinnest at high tide.
It is low tide.
The seaweed has pods of air that are like coffee beans.
Out of the silence an engine approaches.
There are tide lines in the cup.
In the brilliance the boat is a dark chunk, bluntly whittled.
It steadily comes nearer.
It throbs.
It moves across the light and turns white.
It pays out two lines that fan and roll and add their action to the
 surface friction between air and water.
The bay is 1) a continuum and 2) change.
In the boat the figure of a man is ingeniously in scale.
A crow laughs.
The engine throttles.

The boat turns.

The ripples are twisted in a knot that shatters and dissolves.

The small turbulence breaks and melts.

The engine cuts to a rale.

The figure of a man turns, steps and bends and draws out of the dishonored and neglected grave cold-blooded fury entrapped in a lobster pot.

Carapace and claws snapping and thrashing, mottled stormily.

Gaudy shells packed with sweet meat.

The lobsterman turns toward you a face of weathered stone that cracks into a smile.

The price is up because the take is down.

He baits his trap and drops it in the sea.

The asthmatic purr chokes and resumes the stertorous breathing of normalcy.

The boat goes off to grow blue with distance.

The coffee cup has found its way onto the jut of a crag the size of a foot.

The little it holds is cold, bitter, gritty and tastes good.

The air has stopped sliding.

It is a breeze that is more like a wind.

It crumples the bay and stuffs it in a stone pocket.

The bay agitatedly tries to smooth itself out.

If it were tissue paper it would need damp and an iron.

It is a good deal more than damp.

What a lot of water.

A gull barks.

A baby barks back.

Three crows go by about their dark and iridescent business.

The sun is high enough to have its plain daily look of someone who takes in wash.

It dries the laundry.

Suppose I found a bone in the grass and told you it is one of Marc Bloch's?

It would not be true.

No it would not be true and the sea is not his grave.

Noble, great, and good:

It is his cenotaph.

63

"Used Handkerchiefs 5¢"

Clean used ones, of course. Also a dresser scarf, woven with a pattern of pansies looking alternately to right and to left; a pillowcase full of carpet scraps; underdrawers of cambric with an edging of tatting; black— shedding jet and bugles—crêpe, as stuffed with dust and as damp, or as dry, as the wrinkled hand of someone too old to die who dies because to wake up this morning just slipped her mind; bent giant postcards: Mont Pele and a fruitless wonderland of ice prisms, clear water-diluted color chunks: blue; pink and green; sagging brown and metal-threaded tapestry cloth within the gothic arch of a table Motorola hiding a speaker from which once sped Flagstad's more than melodious shriek and, over-enunciated as plums wrapped in papers printed "Biscayne Farms," once trotted, like a quick creek, the news that flaming passengers were falling from the Hindenburg, a voice that left itself a small puddle of kerosene on the linoleum; then there is your face, floating up the stairs, big-eyed into the trash-and-treasures loft from which, finally, dressed for tennis as you came, you go down again with a find in hand: a slab of undyed linen its silverness yellowing like a teaspoon from egg yolk, ironed with too cool an iron so the washing crush marks make a pattern over the weave and, above the thick welt of the hem, a cross-stitched border of spruce and juniper unstylized (unless style is simply to choose) in shades of drab that sink in, or emerge from: the hand towel of today, embroidered forty-some maybe years ago.

Light from Canada

For Charles North

A wonderful freshness, air
that billows like bedsheets
on a clothesline and the clouds
hang in a traffic jam: summer
heads home. Evangeline,
our light is scoured and Nova
Scotian and of a clarity that
opens up the huddled masses
of the stolid spruce so you
see them in their bristling
individuality. The other
day, walking among them, I
cast my gaze upon the ground
in hope of orchids and,
pendant, dead, a sharp shadow
in the shade, a branch gouged
and left me "scarred forever
'neath the eye." Not quite. Not
the cut, but the surprise, and
how, when her dress caught fire,
Longfellow's wife spun
into his arms and in the dying
of its flaring, died. The
irreparable, which changes
nothing that went before
though it ends it. Above the wash
and bark of rumpled water, a gull
falls down the wind to dine
on fish that swim up to do same.

Gulls

Gulls
loudly insist on indefensible rights

Spruce
gather together on spindle shanks

Queen Anne's Lace
tip platters at perilous angles

Hawkweed
all sneeze at the same time

Rocks
go back to sleep

Birches
grunt as they scratch themselves

Stumps
grow old in hospitableness

Moss
free of dandruff

Bunchberries
trotting about

Closed Gentian Distances

A nothing day full of
wild beauty and the
timer pings. Roll up
the silver off the bay
take down the clouds
sort the spruce and
send to laundry marked,
more starch. Goodbye
golden- and silver-
rod, asters, bayberry
crisp in elegance.
Little fish stream
by, a river in water.

September

Swimming in the memorial
park pond smells of a dog

or just wading up and
down on trucked-in sand

oaks do their stuff
a dressy pine

and a kind of a mantid
that inspires respect

it isn't an insect with
only four legs when

its pincers snappily fold
back Danilova/Yastrezemski

that's it in September sun
two of its legs are like—you

know. Arms

Evening Wind

October hangs in grape
bunch lights among the leaves
of a giant tree whose leaves
are not unlike grape leaves:
a plane tree, or a sycamore?
The wind comes up the water
as water from a faucet
runs across a palm, the palm
of your hand, the water turned
on gently or broken into
cool molten woolly glass
by an aerator. And each
responds by his or its
own bending to it, tall tops
of hedge move all in a sideways
way, the grass (it begins
to have its matted resting
up for winter look) is freaked
by shade and quartz grit
bits of light, a pear tree
rocks at its roots and from
the eyebrow curves of branches
or under them flutters absurdly
its leaves like lashes. And I
am troubled by hatred for
the dead. Wind, you don't
blow hard enough, though
rising, in the smoky blue
of evening, mindless and in love.
Or would be if the wind
were not above such thoughts,
above thought, in fact
of course, though coursing,
cool as water, through it.

Slowly

Slowly
the dried-up pond
fills again. The blackish
verge grows spongy. Packed
with seeds of which some
burst unseasonably into
life: kinds of grass in
tufted rays or with blades
folded in purple
cornucopias—
low-growing bedstraw and
others to you nameless—
pushing out for room,
radiating, starring the muck.
A frail gray flower
flies off, an insect
that escaped the first
combing frosts. It's
not—"the fly buzzed"
finding moods, reflectives:
fall
equals melancholy, spring,
get laid: but to turn it all
one way: in repetition, change:
a continuity, the what
of which you are a part.
The clouds are tinted
gray and violet and shred
the blue in other blues.
Each weed as you walk
becomes a rarity.

A Gray Thought

In the sky a gray thought
ponders on three kinds of green:
Brassy tarnished leaves of lilacs
holding on half-heartedly and long
after most turned and fell to make
a scatter rug, warmly, brightly brown.
Odd, that the tattered heart-shapes
on a Persian shrub should stay
as long as the northern needles
of the larch. Near, behind the lilac,
on a trunk, pale Paris green, green
as moonlight, growing on another time scale
a slowness becoming vast as though
all the universe were an atom
of a filterable virus in a head
that turns an eye to smile
or frown or stare into other
eyes: and not of gods, but creatures
whose size begins beyond the sense of size:
lichens, softly colored, hard in durance,
a permanence like rock on a transient tree.
And another green, a dark thick green
to face the winter, laid in layers on
the spruce and balsam or in foxtail
bursts on pine in springy shapes
that weave and pierce
the leafless and unpatterned woods.

Verge

A man cuts brush
and piles it
for a fire where
fireweed will flower
maybe, one day.
All the leaves
are down except
the few that aren't.
They shake or
a wind shakes
them but they
won't go oh
no there goes
one now. No.
It's a bird
batting by.
The small lake,
shrunk, shivers
like a horse
twitching off
flies. Flies
drunkenly stagger
between window
and storm sash.
They hatch, lay,
buzz and die.
The sky grows
gray, goes pale,
bears a whitlow
or splits and
shows a lining
light sea green.
But the lake
is black. Back

of the trees
are other trees
where deer stoop
and step and
the independent skunk
securely waddles. .
An unseen
something stirs
and says: No
snow yet but
it will snow.
The trees sneeze:
You bet it
will, compiling
a white and wordless
dictionary
in which brush
cut, piled and
roofed with glitter
will catch and burn
transparently
bright in white
defining "flame."
So long, north.
See you later
in other weather.

A Stone Knife

December 26, 1969

Dear Kenward,
                    What a pearl
of a letter knife. It's just
the thing I needed, something
to rest my eyes on, and always
wanted, which is to say
it's that of which I
felt the lack but
didn't know of, of no
real use and yet
essential as a button
box, or maps, green
morning skies, islands and
canals in oatmeal, the steam
off oyster stew. Brown
agate, veined as a woods
by smoke that has to it
the watery twist of eel grass
in a quick, rust-discolored
cove. Undulating lines of
northern evening—a Munch
without the angst—a
hint of almost amber:
to the nose, a resinous
thought, to the eye, a
lacquered needle green
where no green is, a
present after-image.
Sleek as an ax, bare
and elegant as a tarn,
manly as a lingam,
November weather petrified,
it is just the thing

to do what with? To
open letters? No, it
is just the thing, an
object, dark, fierce
and beautiful in which
the surprise is that
the surprise, once
past, is always there:
which to enjoy is
not to consume. The un-
recapturable returns
in a brown world
made out of wood,
snow streaked, storm epi-
center still in stone.

The Crystal Lithium

The smell of snow, stinging in nostrils as the wind lifts it from a
    beach
Eye-shuttering, mixed with sand, or when snow lies under the street
    lamps and on all
And the air is emptied to an uplifting gassiness
That turns lungs to winter waterwings, buoying, and the bright
    white night
Freezes in sight a lapse of waves, balsamic, salty, unexpected:
Hours after swimming, sitting thinking biting at a hangnail
And the taste of the—to your eyes—invisible crystals irradiates the
    world
"The sea is salt"
"And so am I"
"Don't bite your nails"
                           and the metal flavor of a nail—are these
    brads?—
Taken with a slight spitting motion from between teeth and
    whanged into place
(Boards and sawdust) and the nail set is ridged with cold
Permanently as marble, always degrees cooler than the rooms of air
    it lies in
Felt as you lay your cheek upon the counter on which sits a blue-
    banded cup
A counter of condensed wintry exhalations glittering infinitesimally
A promise, late on a broiling day in late September, of the cold kiss
Of marble sheets to one who goes barefoot quickly in the snow and
    early
Only so far as the ashcan—bang, dump—and back and slams the
    door:
Too cold to get up though at the edges of the blinds the sky
Shows blue as flames that break on a red sea in which black coals
    float:
Pebbles in a pocket embed the seam with grains of sand
Which, as they will, have found their way into a pattern between
    foot and bedfoot

"A place for everything and everything in its place" how wasteful,
    how wrong
It seems when snow in fat, hand-stuffed flakes falls slow and steady
    in the sea
"Now you see it, now you don't" the waves growl as they grind
    ashore and roll out
At your feet (in boots) a Christmas tree naked of needles
Still wound with swags of tarnishing tinsel, faintly alarming as the
    thought
Of damp electricity or sluggish lightning and for your health-
    desiring pains
The wind awards: Chapped Lips: on which to rub Time's latest
    acquisition
Tinned, dowel-shaped and inappropriately flavored sheep wool fat
A greasy sense-eclipsing fog "I can't see
Without my glasses" "You certainly can't see with them all steamed
    up
Like that. Pull over, park and wipe them off." The thunder of a
    summer's day
Rolls down the shimmering blacktop and mowed grass juice
    thickens the air
Like "Stir until it coats the spoon, remove from heat, let cool and
    chill"
Like this, graying up for more snow, maybe, in which a small flock
Of—sparrows?—small, anyway, dust kitty-colored birds fly up
On a dotted diagonal and there, ah, is the answer:
Starlings, bullies of birdland, lousing up
The pecking order, respecters of no rights (what bird is) unloved
    (oh?)
Not so likeable as some: that's temperate enough and the
    temperature
Drops to rise to snowability of a softness even in its scent of roses
Made of untinted butter frosting: Happy Name Day, Blue Jay,
    staggering
On slow-up wings into the shrunk into itself from cold forsythia
    snarl
And above these thoughts there waves another tangle but one
    parched with heat

And not with cold although the heat is on because of cold settled
     all
About as though, swimming under water, in clearly fishy water, you
Inhaled and found one could and live and also found you altogether
Did not like it, January, laid out on a bed of ice, disgorging
February, shaped like a flounder, and March with her steel bead
     pocketbook,
And April, goofy and under-dressed and with a loud laugh, and
     May
Who will of course be voted Miss Best Liked (she expects it),
And June, with a toothpaste smile, fresh from her flea bath, and
     gross July,
Flexing itself, and steamy August, with thighs and eyes to match,
     and September
Diving into blue October, dour November, and deadly dull
     December which now
And then with a surprised blank look produces from its hand the
     ace of trumps
Or sets within the ice white hairline of a new moon the gibbous
     rest:
Global, blue, Columbian, a blue dull definite and thin as the first
     day
Of February when, in the steamed and freezing capital cash built
Without a plan to be its own best monument its skyline set in stacks
Like poker chips (signed, "Autodidact"), at the crux of a view there
     crosses
A flatcar-trailer piled with five of the cheaper sort of yachts,
     tarpaulined,
Plus one youth in purple pants, a maid in her uniform and an "It's
     not real
Anything" Cossack hat and coat, a bus one-quarter full of strangers
     and
The other familiar fixings of lengthening short days: "He's outgrown
     them
Before you can turn around" and see behind you the landscape of
     the past
Where beached boats bask and terraced cliffs are hung with oranges

Among dark star-gleaming leaves, and, descending the dizzying
	rough stairs
Littered with goat-turd beads—such packaging—you—he—she—
One—someone—stops to break off a bit of myrtle and recite all the
	lines
Of Goethe that come back, and those in French, "*Connais-
	tu . . . ?*" the air
Fills with chalk dust from banged erasers, behind the February
	dunes
Ice boats speed and among the reeds there winds a little frozen
	stream
Where kids in kapok ice-skate and play at Secret City as the sun
Sets before dinner, the snow on fields turns pink and under the
	hatched ice
The water slides darkly and over it a never before seen liquefaction
	of the sun
In a chemical yellow greener than sulphur a flash of petroleum by-
	product
Unbelievable, unwanted and as lovely as though someone you knew
	all your life
Said the one inconceivable thing and then went on washing dishes:
	the sky
Flows with impersonal passion and loosening jet trails (eyes tearing
	from the cold)
And on the beach, between foam frozen in a thick scalloped edging
	so like
Weird cheek-mottling pillowcase embroidery, on the water-darkened
	sand the waves
Keep free of frost, a gull strangles on a length of nylon fishline and
	the dog
Trots proudly off, tail held high, to bury a future dinner among cut
	grass on a dune:
The ice boats furl their sails and all pile into cars and go off to the
	super market
Its inviting foods and cleansers sold under tunes with sealed-in
	memory-flavor

"Hot House Rhubarb" "White Rock Girl" "Citrus Futures" "Cheap
    Bitter Beans" and
In its parking lot vast as the kiss to which is made the most
    complete surrender
In a setting of leaves, backs of stores, a house on a rise admired for
    being
Somewhat older than some others (prettier, too?) a man in a white
    apron embraces a car
Briefly in the cold with his eyes as one might hug oneself for
    warmth for love
—What a paint job, smooth as an eggplant; what a meaty chest,
    smooth as an eggplant
—Is it too much to ask your car to understand you? the converse
    isn't and the sky
Maps out new roads so that, driving at right angles to the wind,
    clouds in ranks
Contrive in diminishing perspective a part of a picture postcard of a
    painting
Over oak scrub where a filling station has: gas, a locked toilet (to
    keep dirt in)
A busted soda pop machine, no maps and "I couldn't tell you *thet*"
    so
The sky empties itself to a color, there, where yesterday's puddle
Offers its hospitality to people-trash and nature-trash in tans and
    silvers
And black grit like that in corners of a room in this or that cheap
    dump
Where the ceiling light burns night and day and we stare at or into
    each
Other's eyes in hope the other reads there what he reads: snow,
    wind
Lifted; black water, slashed with white; and that which is, which is
    beyond
Happiness or love or mixed with them or more than they or less,
    unchanging change,
"Look," the ocean said (it was tumbled, like our sheets), "look in
    my eyes"

Eyes

seta cangiante
eyes that change
changeable as changeable
silk, silk that
refracts
as bearer walks
in sunlight
into shade
from Piazza, say,
San Marco
into sun-charged
shadowy arcade
or under trees
green, green
and between
blue, blue, blue
bluest blue
eyes of un-
weavable color
human eyes, man
size: unsilken
reflections:
hazel, gray-
blue, "tea
ashes" Chinese,
ordinary eyes:
The Big Salty,
shifting restless,
under overcast:
smile, cold, half-
asleep
and deep in August
grass, elms, weeping
birches and all

green, too
green, so green
and the eyes
pick it up and
flash *il raggio verde*
the green ray
al tramonto
sunset flash
the red
reversal: i.e.
green

And in your eyes
your suddenly so
green eyes
the flash holds
steadily and
you smile or
I hope so: it
is not August
yet, *Occhi
di seta cangiante
mi segue?*

The Night

The night is filled with indecisions
To take a downer or an upper
To take a walk
To lie
Down and relax

I order you: RELAX

To face the night
Alight—or dark—the air
Conditioner
The only song:
I love you so
Right now I need you so
So tired and so upset
And yet I mustn't phone:
I didn't know
I touched a wound that never healed
A trauma: wounds will heal
And all I did
Was panic so briefly
On the phone
"Oh baby! you scared me."
No, what you said
First on the phone
Was, "Baby, I'll be right there."
You were. You did. You
Came, it seemed, as fast
As light, you love me so.
I didn't know someone
Once hurt you so,
Went suicidal: head in the oven
Threat—that
Hysteria bit. Not

My trip.
I am not suicidal:
We are strong and
You know it and
Yet
I must sleep
And wait—I
love you so
You will know
I know you do
Already know:
We love each other
So. Good night
My own, my love
My dear, my dearest dear
It's true
We do we
Love each
Other so

Letter to a Friend:
Who Is Nancy Daum?

All things are real
no one a symbol:
curtains (shantung
        silk)
potted palm, a
bust: flat, with pipe—
    M. Pierre Martory
a cut-out by Alex
            Katz:
Dreaming eyes
        and pipe
Contiguous to
en terre cuite
            Marie
Antoinette
her brown and seeming
living curls
and gaze seen as
Reverie: *My Lady*
of My Edgeworth
("Prince Albert in
the can?" "Better
let him out, I . . .")
pipe dream. Some
vitamins; more
Flying Buzzard
        ware:
a silver chain—my
silver chain
from Denmark from
you by way
of London—
(I put it on: cold

and I love
its weight:
   argento
       pessante)
a *sang de boeuf*
       spittoon
or Beauty bowl,
a compact
with a Red Sea
     scene
holding little
pills (Valium
for travel strain),
this French
     lamp
whose stem of
  glass
Lights softly
          up
entwined with
autumn trees
(around the base
    are reeds)
its glass shade
   slightly oiled
as is the dawn
above a swamp
lagoon or fen where
    hunters lurk and
    down marc or cognac
or home-made rotgut
  of their choice,
I—have lost
    my place:
No, here it is:
    Traherne,
Poems, Centuries
  and Three

Thanksgivings,
a book beneath
        the notebook
in which I write.
        Put off the light—
the French lamp
    (signed, somewhere)
And put it on:
the current
            flows.
My heart
beats. Nerves,
        muscles,
the bright invisible
red blood—*sang*
d'homme
  helps (is
that the word?)
        propel
this ball-point
        pen:
black ink is
    not black
        blood.
Two other books:
The Gay
        Insider
—good—*Run*
Little Leather
Boy awaits
assessment
on my Peter Meter.
A trove of glass
    within a
    cabinet
near my
        knees
I wish I were on

my knees
embracing
   yours
       my cheek
against the suiting of
           whatever
suit—about now—
or soon, or late—
("I'm not prompt"
    you said, rueful
         factual
"I" I said, "climb
walls")
O Day!
   literal
and unsymbolic
          day:
silken: gray: sunny:
   in salt and pepper
tweed soot storm:
guide, guard,
      be freely
         pierced
by the steel and
gold-eyed
needle passes—stitches
—of my love, my
        lover,
           our
        love,
his lover—I
        am he—
    (is not
at any tick
each and every life
at hazard: *faites*
vos jeux,
   messieurs)

. . . Where am I?
en route to
a literal
Vermont. It's
time
to
—oh, do this
do that—.
I'll call.
Perhaps we'll
lunch? We
already
said goodbye a
long farewell
for a few weeks'
parting!
My ocean liner,
I am your
tug. "Life
is a bed
of roses:
rugosas,
nor is it always
summer."
Goodbye. Hello.
Kiss
Hug. I
gotta
run. Pierre
Martory,
his semblance,
smokes a St.
Simonian
pipe and thinks
Mme de Sévigné
-type thoughts.
He was, when
posing,

89

perhaps, projecting
A Letter to a Friend.
      (signed)—
all my
—you know—
     ton

        Dopey.
PS The lamp is
   signed, Daum,
     Nancy.
Hence I surmise
   she made
or, at least,
      designed it.
Who *is* Nancy Daum?

We Are Leaves

There are leaves
there are trees
there is a tuba vine
"she"—a voice
she sings in other
words than what
disc grooves carry:
your name your face
our privacy in
hotel rooms with
cheap vodka cheap
quinine water our
nights are days
the morning comes
and goes and we
are pleased or
"who cares?" We
saw that view
of shimmering tall
offices. Today.
Today is muggy
gray—*I* don't
mind: why care?
Today you see
another view
desk and win-
dow ledge, while
mine—my view
that is—is
window ledge
and desk. Do
I miss you?
You know, yes
and I know,

no, you are
so with me
when apart, I
think I under-
stand you and
you me: I'm
happy as a rained-
on leaf or
lettuce in a
crisper. You
love me and I
reciprocate.
The leaves—
it's almost
fall—look
to last for-
ever—they will
come tumbling
down. I'm glad
we are not
leaves, or even
trees whose twigs
mesh. We are—
you are you,
I am I, and
we mesh. And
to ourselves
we speak our
thoughts and
touch and that
is love, isn't
it? What Doc
called, Gen-
ital contact.
And lighter
than a zeppelin
the sense of

touch brushed
lightly one
against the other
we two, together
here among leaves

Await

The scars upon the day
are harsh marks of
tranquility. I scarcely
know where you are:
awake? After lunch, a
Sunday snooze? Is
the ivy weeded yet?
Let the frost do
it its way. Smile, my
dear my dandy, when
you see this. That's
not much to ask, though
no smile on order
is quite the spontaneous
real thing. The day
grinds to a halt all
dusk and yellow rose.
What's a hundred some
miles or so? Or—let's
see—fifty hours?
Time of all things
is most variable, a
seed you plant to see
what in the world
it is a seed of: time,
hours compressed into
a kiss, a lick, or
stretched out by a
train into an endless
rubber band. All we
know is that for such
as us it is not end-
less: is time too to
be found of an atomic

structure? I
would be the last to
know, busily waiting
to see and smile
as you smile and bend
to kiss. Why soon it
will be only forty-
nine hours, cubed in-
visibly like the sec-
tions of a creek.
A record spins,
these keys go clack
why soon I'll see
you and soon you'll
see me. I can enjoy
the here and now
but, wind shivering
clear day, I live
and love to anticipate
my hands on you and
yours on me, the
hours flow by and
a white gull is
black against
November evening
light, expressed,
it seems, from
late yellow grapes.

Steaming Ties

Steaming ties, cutting rue
when I'm alone it's hard
at times to know how unalone
I am, loved by you. We phone.
A heavy talk on real estate, you
own land. I don't. Once did.
Sold it for a trip:
Italy, France, two years:
bye bye, Arkansas homestead.
Still and all on this radiant
September leaf light day
the leaves lit it seems or
seeming is from insides,
lovely inwardness of leaves
that dapple themselves with shade,
and all, and still I have a
place to lay my head
on you, oh, anywhere:
I'm no body bigot but
sometimes even yet or now, I
mean, I forget for a few
sad minutes how unalone I
am, steaming ties you gave
me, ties are, yes even ties,
are silk and real. Your
voice to me is silk and rustles.
We will meet, soon, not
soon enough. I remember I'm
unalone, you are with me,
salty sneezes off Atlantic
Ocean, there, where you are
here, in my heart and head
you blend in softly bright

September: you are moonrise
you are pain, you're mine
and I am yours, steaming
out silk ties, they bind

Watching You

Watching you sleep
a thing you do so well
no shove no push
on the sliding face
of sleep as on
the deep a sea bird
of a grand wingspread
trusts what it knows
and I who rumple crumple
and mash (snore) amble
and ankle about wide
awake, wanting to fold,
loving to watch sleep
embodied in you my
warm machine that draws
me back to bed
and you who turn
all toward me
to love and seduce
me back to sleep "You
said 9:30, now it's
10:" you
don't seem to care
cold coffee (sugar,
no milk) about time:
you never do, never
get roiled the way
I do "Should I nag
you or shut up? If
you say, I will"
always be
glad to return to
that warm turning

to me in that
tenderest moment
of my nights,
and more, my days.

Letter Poem #3

The night is quiet
as a kettle drum
the bullfrog basses
tuning up. After
swimming, after sup-
per, a Tarzan movie,
dishes, a smoke. One
planet and I
wish. No need
of words. Just
you, or rather,
us. The stars tonight
in pale dark space
are clover flowers
in a lawn the expanding
universe in which
we love it is
our home. So many
galaxies and you my
bright particular,
my star, my sun, my
other self, my bet-
ter half, my one

FROM

Hymn to Life

[1 9 7 4]

Beautiful Funerals

Who lives in the biggest, whitest house in town?
The mortician, man.
Who's the man with all that greenery, the shrubs, the velvet turf,
who's the gink they all make fun of
in tones not untouched with awe?
They will indeed be calling on Frank C.
Campbell (Or someone like him: let's call him Frank)
in their Hour of Greatest Need.
He's no four-flusher,
kind of a con man (ask Jessica, Jessica knows).
Has he a fish eye?
Not necessarily.
Is he a creep?
Not on my street.
Is he a ghoul?
Oh get lost.
He's a Rotarian: why not?
A VIP in the VFW—
watch it, mac, so's my brother.
He's the man who can lay it out, rich and ready,
and some people rate it
no matter how they choose to go:
as mulch or ashes
(make mine mulch):
he is the mortician man, I don't
chew my cookies twice
though needs must, I will
call on Frank today,
and to him say, man to man,
                    Libby Holman's
                    Dead and gone
                    Way over Jordan water
                    God loves his children
                    She was and is

His daughter:
Forget the rest.
Libby Holman—
She was and is:
You were and are—
Totally great.
Libby Holman
Is laid to rest.
("Did she shoot him?"
For Pete's sake,
she was acquitted:
isn't that enough?
And don't start
whining, "We will
never know," you
busted
Broadway
Butterfly)
She will greet Louis Armstrong
at the gate
when he stomps in playing
" 'Cornet Chop Suey'
'Potato Head Blues'
and in deeper and
more deliberate fashion
'West End Blues' and
'Tight Like That' " (thank
you, Mr. John C. Wilson).
Lay it on, Frank,
lined in quilted satin
in husky hues
of blues: fittings
of bronze *doré*, for
a touch theatrical
steamer-trunk type
decals on the hand-
rubbed ebony

THE LITTLE SHOW,
MOANIN' LOW, an
air from THE HOUSE
OF BERNARDA ALBA:
"But these are
grave matters."
"Sez who."
When a soul departs
on its wingèd flight
hit the vox humana
and let it rip: they
"burst out singing"
'Bye Bye Blackbird'
right at the graveside
for Florence Mills.
Vachel Lindsay, lead
Miss Holman by the hand
kindly re-introduce
her in that promised land
(they surely met) to
Messers O'Hara,
the poet Frank, and
John, the delicate author
of *Imagine Kissing Pete.*
Put silver slippers
on golden feet, call
on the choir of the
great torch singers:
Marion Harris, will
she be there? You
know it. As they
walk in meadows of
lifting mist or stop
for a quickie in a
honky-tonk saloon
all the reality
the wonderful fakery

of props and flats,
the shifting machinery
of a musical's scenery,
slap on a baby
spot and make it *blue*.
Miss Holman, shortly,
is about to sing.

Frank O'Hara chats
apart with Carole Lombard
and James Dean while
John O'Hara makes
whoopee at a dignified
gait with Scott Fitz-
gerald and Nathanael
West. And where is
Papa? Honking where
the wild goose goes:
Zelda shimmies
in that world apart
where life to her
is a sazerac. Francis
Poulenc pounds
out *Les Funérailles*.
Libby Holman is
laid to rest.
Forget the rest.
"Miss Holman . . ."
(Povla Frisch is polite
as she is able to
Mary Garden) "presently
will sing." John
Latouche hands out
his smile extending.
The house lights darken:
immortal stuff shuffles
back from the *entr'acte*.

A trumpet in a derby hat,
a soft slide, the sax-
ophones. The house
goes black. Stage left,
the eternal flame. *L'Arc
de Triomphe, la ville
lumière.* In the night
rises a moon-blue spot:
someone is leaning
on the great stone trophy.
She is wearing what they
wore, oh, back then,
a Kiki outfit, with
tam and pumps. She
leans against a fake
it is all so real,
this artifice, not
a leaf is heard:
the mood, deep indigo.
Libby Holman prepares
to sing in a husky
untrained baritone.
Change the scene. It's
an after concert. She is,
as they say, perched
on a table edge, one
foot adangle. She wears—
let it be sable, con-
versing with Montgomery
Clift. At the keys,
Lorenz Hart (her son
is there), and
then she sings it,
her latest number,
"Dignity
in Dark Glasses."

Our Father

This morning view
is very plain: thou art
in Heaven: modern
brick, plate glass, unhallowèd,
as yet, by time,
yet Thy Name
blesses all: silver tanks
of propane gas, the sky,
Thy will,
is lucent blue, French
gray and cream,
is done: the night
on earth
no longer needs
the one white street globe light
as the light, it is
in Heaven.
Give us this day
—and a Friday
13th, August '71,
at that:
our daily bread
and breakfast
(Product 19,
an egg, perchance: the hen-fruit,
food and symbol)
and forgive us our
trespasses
too numerous
to name—as we
forgive our debtors: "pay
me when you can:
I don't take
interest"

how green
the grass! so many
flowering weeds
Your free
will has freely
let us name: dandy-
lion (*pisse-en-lit*)
and, clover
(O Trinity)
it is
a temptation
to list them all,
all I know, that is:
the temptation
to show off—to
make a show
of knowing more,
than, in fact, I
know, is very real:
as real as a twelve-
pane window sash
one pane slivered
by a crack, a flash,
a mountain line
that stays
to praise
Thee,
Your Name and Your
    Creation
let me surrender
ever—
poets do: it
is their way
and deliver me
from evil
and the Three
Illusions

of the Will—
for the power
that flows electrically
in me is thine
O glorious central,
O plant,
O dynamo!
and the glory
of this cool a.m.
now
all
silver, blue
and white.

Poem

This beauty that I see
—the sun going down
scours the entangled
and lightly henna
withys and the wind
whips them as it
would ship a cloud—
is passing so swiftly
into night. A moon,
full and flat, and stars
a freight train passing
passing it is the sea
and not a train. This
beauty that collects
dry leaves in pools
and pockets and goes
freezingly, just able
still to swiftly flow
it goes, it goes.

To Frank O'Hara

For Don Allen

And now the splendor of your work is here
so complete, even
"a note on the type"
yes, total, even the colophon

and now people you never met will meet
and talk about your work.
So witty, so sad,
so you: even your lines have

a broken nose. And in the crash
of certain chewed-up words
I see you again dive
into breakers! How you scared

us, no, dazzled us swimming
in an electric storm
which is what you were
more lives than a cat

dancing, you had a feline
grace, poised on the balls
of your feet ready
to dive and

all of it, your poems,
compressed into twenty years.
How you charmed, fumed,
blew smoke from your nostrils

like a race horse that
just won the race

112

steaming, eager to run
only you used words.

Stay up all night? Who wants to sleep?
It is not your voice I hear
it is your words I see
foam flecks and city girders

as once from a crosstown bus
I saw you waiting a cab in light rain
(drizzle) as once you
gave me a driving lesson and the radio

played *The Merry Widow*. It broke us up.
As once under the pie plate tree
(Paulonia)
it broke you up to read Sophie Tucker

—with the *Times* in a hammock—
had a gold tea service. "It's way out
on the nut," she said, "for service,
but it was my dream."

Unlike Joubert

Lying on the bed in the afternoon
but not "in a pink dressing gown"
in red pajamas and a yellow bathrobe
—flannel pajamas and a terry-cloth bathrobe—
and for a moment, a flicked-off bit
of a moment, succeeding where Joubert
failed: to think nothing; but on
second thought, failing, as it was not
by intention, nor is it certain that
there was even the shaved off edge
of a flick between the thought and
the next thought, that there had been
thought between them. All that is
clear on this shadowless day under
a sky like a shadow is that the first
thought was gray, a harshly bright
blue-gray, a piece of too highly colored
slate, while the second was gray
as some roses are, or hair you see
was once red, a gray with the charm
and warmth to it of an intimate and
not overly cozy room, one with woodwork
by Pajou, or like worn upholstery, or
your first biplane. As different as
day from night, and as alike,
just as their connective—the nothing which
may not have been—was also a gray,
creamier, lighter, and shifty-eyed
as the sky or a big flat button
cut out of a seashell, the polished
off husk of an oyster, perhaps:
subtle days in winter when thought
sinks down in the presence of an absence.

Eyes at the Window

The eyes at the window are Norma Shearer's
at the train window. Kaspar Hauser
waits at the station. He has something
he urgently wishes to say
to Alexander Hamilton's whore.
The veiled lady is Burr's daughter
under the grapes in Alexandria, Virginia.
Robert Schuyler, the great defaulter,
at a place on the plains meets
the man who robbed a Rothschild.
They set up shop in Minnesota.
The bones though are those of Ambrose Bierce.
The trap door is lowered before the door.
A tap on the door.
Amy Robsart comes to the door.
The bones though are Ambrose Bierce's.

The Veiled Lady has a story to tell: haven't you, too, old tree, new
house? Or coincidence in a name, the glamor and cash of crime
without the blood and reparation. Or to be greatness' sordid secret,
object or wish—to be purely a thought! And who never felt himself
the inarticulate stranger? A wildman without a wood. Or dreamt a
Minnesota or midnight under the warm grapes and the sound of an
ambling horse comes over the wall. And if Amy had looked before
she stepped "things might have turned out very differently from what
in fact they did" says Norman F. Cantor of Brandeis University. Nor
is Bierce's death stranger than another.

>   The pair of buttocks balancing
>   up the stairs are Norma Shearer's. The eyes
>   on them are Conrad Veidt's.
>   "The fate of an empire held
>   in a woman's hand!" drums thunder.
>   What a lot of malarkey. But Kaspar Hauser:

was he a fraud? Nor was the Veiled Lady
so to herself. It is easy
to respect such privacy and prefer
not knowing. Thieves are tedious
and about Amy it is all conjecture. Still,
this morning they came together:
they have come together this still morning
at a railway station where yuccas
grow wild in cinders and the station wall
is of oystershells embedded in stucco
on an almost destroyed island
upon which March prepares to lay a hand.
Eyes at the window, womanly
mysteries, jabbering stranger,
consanguineous disreputability,
Bohemian Bierce lighting out like Huck,
and Amy Robsart, a thought in space,
hung
there briefly. The thought
though is Walter Scott's.

Shimmer

The pear tree that last year
was heavy-laden this year
bears little fruit. Was
it that wet spring we had?
All the pear tree leaves
go shimmer, all at once. The
August sun blasts down
into the coolness from the
ocean. *The New York Times*
is on strike. My daily
fare! I'll starve! Not
quite. On my sill, balls
of twine wrapped up in
cellophane glitter. The
brown, the white and one
I think you'd call écru.
The sunlight falls partly
in a cup: it has a blue
transfer of two boys, a
dog and a duck and says,
"Come Away Pompey." I
like that cup, half
full of sunlight. Today
you could take up the
tattered shadows off
the grass. Roll them
and stow them. And collect
the shimmerings in a
cup, like the coffee
here at my right hand.

Greenwich Avenue

In the evening of a brightly
unsunny day to watch back-lighted
buildings through the slits
between vertical strips of blinds
and how red brick, brick painted
red, a flaky white, gray or
those of no color at all take
the light though it seems only
above and behind them so what
shows below has a slight evening
"the day—sob—dies" sadness and
the sun marches on. It isn't like that
on these buildings, the colors which
seem to melt, to bloom and go and
return, do so in all reality. Go
out and on a cross street briefly
a last sidelong shine catches
the faces of brick and enshadows
the grout: which the eye sees only
as a wash of another diluted color
over the color it thinks it knows
is there. Most things, like the sky,
are always changing, always the same.
Clouds rift and a beam falls
into a cell where a future saint
sits scratching. Or a wintry
sun shows as a shallow pan of red
above the Potomac, below Mount Vernon,
and the doctor from Philadelphia
nods and speaks of a further bleeding.

Just Before Fall

In the quiet spaces between equinoctial gales
silence sparkles
or in a spruce woods
shows as trunks striped light and dark
seen between each other
all the same, each different:
a woods stripped of its lower branches
that lie loosely stacked by the path through it:
mossed, lichened, decaying.

The sun sits in the sky like a painting of it.
The asters bend to a breeze
it is beneath the dignity of woodier plants to notice.
Goldenrod stands in spires
or another kind, that points in Indian sign language:
"This way."

Early in the afternoon the moon slides up the sky
as the sun goes west
its light sits weightlessly
on chokecherry and elderberry brush.
They look held down
and drawn up by it
as a speedboat flees from the furrow
that seems to propel it
through illusions of green
made by black trees reflected on shattering water
shaping itself.
Marvelous universal energy,
expressed in a stellar stillness!
The Milky Way unfurled
last night above the house
and the Pleiades
to the eye faintly cried,

"The best way to see stars
is to look a little to one side"
a universe in its net of space
running down, winding up, going on

Buttered Greens

Sunshine
makes shade
acid blue
leaf work
of elms
they fell first
blown under
a big plane
tree lying
on tuftedness
the pattern
of its later
shedding. In
fields rise
as of them-
selves, houses.
Don't "tsk
tsk" men and
habitations
are nature
too in waves
of concourse
disposable
cities give
a sense
of certainty.
"But! All
alike! How
Levittown!"
Why not
alike as
leaves which
have not
free will:

have you?
You have
you use it
unknowingly
as a house
leaf plastered
after a storm
its white
stained in
leaf marks
elm, plane
tree, a
man's will
turns in
upon it-
self if,
or rather
is it to
use or to
relax it?
Letting what
comes, go
and go in
dark, in
green and
acid blue
that fumes
as he frets
about lit-
tering houses
inside all
is not con-
tent, yet
the chance
of it is
there, free
leaves fall

and the will
stirs and
turns out
from it-
self, housed
in disposable
rib cages
(the heart
thumps), in
disposable
houses, wood
ribbed and
glazed to
flash back
buttered
green, what
it means:
leavings and
the permanence
of return
"I'll be
back by
night" wind
raking leaves
from trees
until: and
then: to-
morrow. It
is strange
and easy,
the will
exercised
within
its wind-
cleared and
cleaned
range, the

"that" not
understood
too well
the will
will heal
what hurt
though that
was what
was meant:
to do
and undo
what's
done be-
tween the
flash and
fall of
turning,
as the year
returns in
its ad-
vance to
take again
what it
last took
and what
it takes
brings back:
all done
not by
us or for
us but
with us
and within
the body
of a house
the frame
of wood or

bone it is
much the
same

In Wiry Winter

The shadow of a bird
upon the yard upon
a house; it's gone.
Through a pane a
beam like a warm hand
laid upon an arm.
A thin shell, trans-
parent, blue: the
atmosphere in which
to swim. Brr. A
cold plunge. The bird
is back. All the same,
to swim, plunging
upward, arms as wings,
into calm cold. Warm
within the act,
treading air, a shadow
on the yard.
Or floating, gliding,
a shadow on the roofs
and drives, in action
warm, the shadow cold
but brief. To swim
in air. No. Not in
this wiry winter air.
A beam comes in the
glass, a hand to
warm an arm. A hand
upon the glass
finds it a kind
of ice. The shadow
of a bird less cold.
Window, miraculous
contrivance; sun-

hot wires in
meshed cold.
The bird goes
quick as a wish
to swim up
and cast, like
it, a shadow
on the years.

So Good

Sing to me
weather about
one bird
peck, pecking
on bleached
winter grass.
March is here
like a granny
a child doesn't
like to kiss:
the farm smell,
a chill sweet-
ness. He'll
get over it.
March will pass
other birds
will sing in
other weather
time twists my
bent back.
A common cold.
And for no
reason my eyes
and the sky
fill with
tears. Two
kinds of
weather and
if you never
cry, well,
then you don't.
Snow that
turns to rain,
pain, physical

and emotive, too
these pass. They
once weren't
here: they'll go
as Granny went
embanked in flowers
so long ago, so
cold a cheek to
ask a child
to kiss. "Those
birds," she
would have said,
"are starlings.
They came from
England." Or
"This is a
monarch butter-
fly." Or, "That
is flypaper. Flies
spread germs."
Or. No. It
was all too long
ago and any
tears are for
the sullen day
suddenly so like
the inner life
that gutters,
burns and smokes.
Light the lights.
The day is dark
and where do
the starlings
sleep at night?
Good night, Granny,
so truly good.

October

Books litter the bed,
leaves the lawn. It
lightly rains. Fall has
come: unpatterned, in
the shedding leaves.

The maples ripen. Apples
come home crisp in bags.
This pear tastes good.
It rains lightly on the
random leaf patterns.

The nimbus is spread
above our island. Rain
lightly patters on un-
shed leaves. The books
of fall litter the bed.

A blue towel

went with us to the beach.
You drove the Green Bomb,
your panel truck. Sand
dunes and signs: "No Parking
Between Signs." "Prohibited
On This Beach . . . Hard Ball . . .
Intoxication . . . Bonfires . . ."
Mist, and filterable sun.
Oh breakers, and leaping
spume! We spread the towel
where we could lie and watch
the fierce and molten wonder
of the water. You wore blue
trunks, and took off a
striped Roman shirt and kicked
off Gucci loafers (and you
think I'm hard on clothes).
We lay and watched and
smoked. I studied sand
and the sand-like freckles
on your back and, smaller
than small, one blackhead
(later removed). And thought
beach thoughts: after sex,
man is sad, some Roman said.
Did he mean, because the
pleasure's over? It's the
day after last night and I
am anything but sad. Quiet
content, a little tired: we
do go on so. Then we walked,
you in surf, I on scoured
sand, firm, and running to

escape the waves that almost
got my sneakers. Then we
walked back. Your trunks
were partly wet, as though
you'd pissed your pants. "I
think," you said, "I'll go
in after all." Then there
you were, bobbing in breakers,
leaping high to ride their
great and breaking crested
curl. It scared me (a
lousy swimmer) just a
little. "That's the way,"
you said when you came
out, "I like it. It's
almost warm enough." I saw
your chest and side be-
side me, pearled with
water drops. The mist
moved off. We sat and sunned
—it was late, no tan today—
and watched the repetitions
of the sea, each one
different from the last,
and saw how a log was
almost hurled ashore then
taken back, slipping north
along the shore. The flies
were something else. "These
insects are too much: let's
go back." The blue towel
and your trunks I hung out
on the line. You took a
shower. I made drinks. Quiet
ecstasy and sweet content,
why are not all days like
you? Happy with someone,

132

and that someone you, to-
gether on a blue towel
on sand beside the sea.

The Bluet

And is it stamina
that unseasonably freaks
forth a bluet, a
Quaker lady, by
the lake? So small,
a drop of sky that
splashed and held,
four-petaled, creamy
in its throat. The woods
around were brown,
the air crisp as a
Carr's table water
biscuit and smelt of
cider. There were frost
apples on the trees in
the field below the house.
The pond was still, then
broke into a ripple.
The hills, the leaves that
have not yet fallen
are deep and oriental
rug colors. Brown leaves
in the woods set off
gray trunks of trees.
But that bluet was
the focus of it all: last
spring, next spring, what
does it matter? Unexpected
as a tear when someone
reads a poem you wrote
for him: "It's this line
here." That bluet breaks
me up, tiny spring flower
late, late in dour October.

Standing and Watching

Standing and watching
through the drizzle
how the mist and further
edge of pond merge
into one grayness, a color
called drained-of-blueness.

Standing and watching
how the maple leaves
fall, lightly pelted by
drizzle, and turn
in air, to lie scattered,
drained, not quite of color there.

The Green Door

"We could try it,"
Ralph says to Harold.
The men are working
on the ell, a new
wing for an old house.

Out the window, the land
drops rapidly away
in wooded undulations and
fields and one larch
there turns to its own gold.

Out another window, one
bare tree laces its limbs
next to a maple which
still has half its leaves
on. Maple gold, not larch.

A plane goes over.
Ralph and Harold hammer
somewhere beyond a
green baize door. Even
the door has its story.

Many moist days, nor
is the end in sight.
I haven't seen the beaver.
The pond, the air, is still:
only the plane, only the hammer.

The Day

The day is gray
as stone: the stones
embedded in the
dirt road are chips
of it. How dark it
gets here in the
north when a cold
front moves in. The
wind starts up. It
keens around the
house in long
sharp sighs at
windows. More
leaves come down
and are borne
sidewise. In the
woods a flock
of small white
moths fluttered,
flying, like the
leaves. The wind
in trees, a
heavy surge, drowns
out the water-
fall: from here,
a twisted thread.
Winter knocks at
the door. Don't
let it in. But
those shivering,
hovering late
moths,
the size of big
snowflakes: what

were they doing
there, so late
in the year? Had
they laid their
eggs, and fluttered
in the then still
woods, aware of
the coming wind,
the storm, their
end? But they
were beautiful,
there in the woods,
frantic with life.

The Walk

Out of shape,
my legs ache
going down
this steep
hill. I hear
the water
rushing down
beside me
through the
trees. Has
the creek
a name? It
somewhere joins
the brown Winooski.
The ferns
the frost
has killed and
curled: another
kind it hasn't.
One dandelion
a frayed
sun in sun-
light that
lights up the
empurpled
blackberry
leaves. Remember
when you picked
them? A dog
and a friendly
voice that calls,
"He's friendly."
One horse in
a field that

stands stock-
still, soaking
up the sun.
And twelve
cows, each doing
something dif-
ferent: munching,
lying down.
The way a
white house
takes late light
and turns it
back. A tumbled
shed, once red,
with missing
windows and
gear stowed
inside. A
long and
steady climb
I've made before:
now my legs
ache, I only
want to reach
the top to where
the road ambles
down through
woods between
tumbled field-
stone walls. This
land once all
was cleared. The
sun is on
the trees on
the far side
of the pond
on which they

in image lie.
The cabin, then
the house. Clear
air, warm
Indian summer
sun, the mosses
that I saw, and
delicate white
lichens, the
trees that make
it and the
trees that don't.
Soon blue snow
will shroud it
all: why take
a long walk
with aching legs?
For fun? Why
not? I can-
not tell you
all I saw,
but won't for-
get the deer
slot stamped
in the muddy
road. I love
their white
scuts when they
bound away,
deer at horseplay.

Awoke

Awoke to rain
and mist, down
there in Gospel
Hollow: a cloud
that frayed and
flowed uphill
as the drizzling
day wore on. We're
not that high
up and yet to-
day we were
above a cloud.
I like that,
high on Apple
Hill beside
the pond where
you watch the
beaver and how
he uses his
tail to turn.
"And then," you
said, "he vanished."

Afterward

Then it snowed. I
saw it when I let
the dog out into
the dark yard, fat
damp flakes, ag-
glomerations of
many flakes. A
white awakening,
a drive to North-
field, picking up
mended quilts from
the quilt lady. You
used the four-
wheel drive on
the mud-slick hill.
The branches bent
under their first
winter weight: it
wasn't pretty, a
thawing snow seldom
is, but it wasn't
ugly, too. In the
morning we left, all
the weeds hoar-
frosted on the hill:
a glittering gray
sheen on brown. In
the valley, the snow
was already gone. Now,
New York, in a tempest
of rain, stalled cabs
and cars, neon re-
flected on asphalt:

I like that, too.
Dreaming of a white
Vermont, scratched
by alders and firs.

Hymn to Life

The wind rests its cheek upon the ground and feels the cool damp
And lifts its head with twigs and small dead blades of grass
Pressed into it as you might at the beach rise up and brush away
The sand. The day is cool and says, "I'm just staying overnight."
The world is filled with music, and in between the music, silence
And varying the silence all sorts of sounds, natural and man-made:
There goes a plane, some cars, geese that honk and, not here, but
Not so far away, a scream so rending that to hear it is to be
Never again the same. "Why, this is hell." Out of the death
    breeding
Soil, here, rise emblems of innocence, snowdrops that struggle
Easily into life and hang their white enamel heads toward the dirt
And in the yellow grass are small wild crocuses from hills goats
Have cropped to barrenness. The corms come by mail, are planted,
Then do their thing: to live! To live! So natural and so hard
Hard as it seems it must be for green spears to pierce the all-but-
Frozen mold and insist that they too, like mouse-eared chickweed,
Will live. The spears lengthen, the bud appears and spreads, its
Seed capsule fattens and falls, the green turns yellowish and withers
Stretched upon the ground. In Washington, magnolias were in bud.
In Charlottesville early bulbs were up, brightening the muck.
    Tomorrow
Will begin another spring. No one gets many, one at a time,
    like a long-
Awaited letter that one day comes. But it may not say
    what you hoped
Or distraction robs it of what it once would have meant.
    Spring comes
And the winter weather, here, may hold. It is arbitrary, like the
    plan
Of Washington, D.C. avenues and circles in asphalt web and no
One gets younger: which is not, for the young, true, discovering
    new
Freedoms at twenty, a relief not to be a teen-ager anymore.
    One of us

Had piles, another water on the knee, a third a hernia—a
    strangulated
Hernia is one of life's less pleasant bits of news—and only
One, at twenty, moved easily through all the galleries to pill
Free sleep. Oh, it's not all that bad. The sun shines on my hand
And the myriad lines that crisscross tell the story of nearly fifty
Years. Sorry, it's too long to relate. Once, when I was young, I
Awoke at first light and sitting in a rocking chair watched the sun
Come up beyond the houses across the street. Another time I stood
At the cables of a liner and watched the wake turning and
Turning upon itself. Another time I woke up and in a bottle
On a chest of drawers the thoughtful doctor had left my tonsils. I
Didn't keep them. The turning of the globe is not so real to us
As the seasons turning and the days that rise out of early gray
—The world is all cut-outs then—and slip or step steadily down
The slopes of our lives where the emotions and needs sprout. "I
Need you," tree, that dominates this yard, thick-waisted, tall
And crook-branched. Its bark scales off like that which we forget:
Pain, an introduction at a party, what precisely happened umpteen
Years or days or hours ago. And that same blue jay returns,
    or perhaps
It is another. All jays are one to me. But not the sun
    which seems at
Each rising new, as though in the night it enacted
    death and rebirth,
As flowers seem to. The roses this June will be different roses
Even though you cut an armful and come in saying,
    "Here are the roses,"
As though the same blooms had come back, white freaked with red
And heavily scented. Or a cut branch of pear blooms
    before its time,
"Forced." Time brings us into bloom and we wait, busy, but wait
For the unforced flow of words and intercourse and sleep and
    dreams
In which the past seems to portend a future which is just more
Daily life. The cat has a ripped ear. He fights, he fights all
The tom cats all the time. There are blood gouts on a velvet seat.

Easily sponged off: but these red drops on a book of Stifter's, will
I remember and say at some future time, "Oh, yes, that was the day
Hodge had a torn ear and bled on the card table?" Poor
Hodge, battered like an old car. Silence flows into my mind. It
Is spring. It is also still really winter. Not a day when you say,
"What a beautiful spring day." A day like twilight or evening when
You think, "I meant to watch the sun set." And then comes on
To rain. "You've got to take," says the man at the store, "the rough
With the smooth." A window to the south is rough with rain-drops
That, caught in the screen, spell out untranslatable glyphs. A story
Not told: so much not understood, a sight, an insight, and
     you pass on,
Another day for each day is subjective and there is a totality of days
As there are as many to live it. The day lives us and in exchange
We it: after snowball time, a month, March, of fits
     and starts, winds,
Rain, spring hints and wintry arrears. The weather pays its check,
Like quarreling in a D.C. hotel, "I won't quarrel about it, but
     I made
No local calls." Strange city, broad and desolating, monuments
Rearing up and offices like monuments and crowds lined up to see
The White House inside. "We went to see the White House. It
     was lovely."
Not so strange though as the cemetery with guttering flame and
Admirals and generals with bigger gravestones than the lesser fry
Below Lee's house, false marble pillars and inside all so
Everyday, in every room a shawl tossed untidily upon a chair or bed
Created no illusion of lived-in-ness. But the periwinkles do, in beds
That flatten and are starred blue-violet, a retiring flower loved,
It would seem, of the dead, so often found
     where they congregate. A
Quote from Aeschylus: I forget. All, all is forgotten gradually and
One wonders if these ideas that seem handed down
     are truly what they were?
An idea may mutate like a plant, and what was once
     held basic truth

Become an idle thought, like, "Shall we plant
     some periwinkles there
By that bush? They're so to be depended on." The wind
     shakes the screen
And all the raindrops on it streak and run in stems. It's colder.
The crocuses close up. The snowdrops are brushed with mud.
     The sky
Colors itself rosily behind gray-black and the rain falls through
The basketball hoop on a garage, streaking its backboard
     with further
Trails of rust, a lovely color to set with periwinkle violet-blue.
And the trees shiver and shudder in the light rain blasts from off
The ocean. The street, wet, reflects the breakup of the clouds
On its face, driving over sky with a hissing sound. The car
Slides slightly and in the west appear streaks of different green:
A lid lifted briefly on the spring. Then the moon burns through
Racing clouds, its aureole that of rings of oil on water in a harbor
Bubbling up from an exhaust. Clear the sky, beside a rim of moon
Three stars and only three and one planet. So under lilacs unleaved
Lie a clump of snowdrops and one purple crocus. Purple,
     a polka-dotted
Color little girls are fond of: "See my new dress!" and she twirls
On one foot. Then, crossed, bursts into tears. Smiles and rain, like
These passing days in which buds swell, unseen as yet, waiting
For the elms to color their furtheroutmost twigs, only the willow
Gleams yellow. Life is hard. Some are strong, some weak, most
Untested. These useless truths blow about the yard the day after
Rain the soft sunlight making softer shadows on the faded lawn.
The world looks so old in the spring, laid out under the sky. One
Gull coasts by, unexpected as a kiss on the nape of the neck. These
Days need birds and so they come, a flock of ducks, and a bunch of
Small fluffy unnamed balls that hide in hedges and make a racket.
"The gift of life," as though, existing in expectancy and then
Someone came up and said, "Here," or, "Happy Birthday."
     It is more
Mysterious than that, pierced by blue or running in the rain
Or simply lying down to read. Writing a postponed
     letter which may

Bring no pleasure: arduous truths to tell. And if you thought
    March was bad
Consider April, early April, wet snow falling into blue squills
That underneath a beech make an illusory lake, a haze of blue
With depth to it. That is like pain, ordinary household pain,
Like piles, or bumping against a hernia. All the signs are set for A-
    OK.
A day to visit the National Gallery—Velázquez, Degas—but, and
What a but, with water on the knee "You'll need a wheelchair,
    Mummy."
Coasting among the masterpieces, of what use are they?
    Angel with a
Hurdy-Gurdy or this young man in dun clothes who holds
    his hat so that
The red lining shows and glows. And in the sitting room people sit
And rest their feet and talk of where they've been, motels and
    Monticello,
Dinner in the Fiji Room. Someone forgets a camera. Each
    day forgetting:
What is there so striking to remember? The rain stops. April shines
A little, stormily, the ocean off there makes its freight-car noise
Or rattles with catarrh and asks to have its nose wiped. Gray
    descends.
An illuminous penetration of unbright light that seeps and coats
The ragged lawn and spells out bare spots and winter
    fallen branches.
Yardwork. And now the yardwork is over (it is never over), today's
Stint anyway. Odd jobs, that stretch ahead, wide and mindless as
Pennsylvania Avenue or the bridge to Arlington, crossed
    and recrossed
And there the Lincoln Memorial crumbles. It looks
    so solid: it won't
Last. The impermanence of permanence, is that all there is?
    To look
And see the plane tree, its crooked branches brush the ground, rear
In its age, older than any of us, destined, if all goes well with it,
To outlast us all. Does one then resent the plane tree, host
To cardinals? I hear them call. Plaintively, in the mating season.

Why should a white city dog my thoughts? Vast, arid,
   a home to many,
So strange in its unamiability. Stony city laid out
   on an heroic plan,
Why are you there? Various answers present themselves, likely
As squills. It doesn't really matter, for instance, to miss the spring.
For this is spring, this mud and swelling fruit-tree buds, furred
On the apple trees. And yet it still might snow: it's been known
Falling like cherry blossom petals around the Reflecting Pool,
   a sight
To see. And there are sights to hear, music from a
   phonograph, pop
Or classical, please choose one or both. It doesn't matter.
   What matters
Is how the light becomes entrapped in a dusty screen, masking out
The view into the depths of the garage where cars are stalled
   like oxen.
Day, suddenly sunny and warming up for more, I would like
   to stroke you
As one strokes a cat and feels the ridgy skull beneath the fur
   and tickles
It behind its ears. The cat twists its head and moves it
   toward your fingers
Like the lifting thighs of someone fucked, moving up
   to meet the stroke.
The sun strokes all now in this zone, reaching in
   through windows to jell
Glue in jars (that takes time)—may I send you a warmed bottle of
   Pliobond?
It is on this desk and—here's the laugh—I don't know
   who put it there.
"This is something he will like, or use." Meantime, those branches
   go
Ungathered up. I hate fussing with nature and would like
   the world to be
All weeds. I see it from the train, citybound, how
   the yuccas and chicory

150

Thrive. So much messing about, why not leave the world
        alone? Then
There would be no books, which is not to be borne. Willa Cather
        alone is worth
The price of admission to the horrors of civilization. Let's
        make a list.
The greatest paintings. Preferred orchestral conductors. Nostalgia
        singers.
The best, the very best, roses. After learning all their names—Rose
de Rescht, Cornelia, Pax—it is important to forget them. All these
Lists are so much dirty laundry. Sort it out fast and send to laundry
Or hurl into washing machine, add soap and let'er spin.
        The truth is
That all these household tasks and daily work—up the street
        two men
Install an air conditioner—are beautiful. Flowers and
        machines that people
Love: the boy who opts for trade school while white-collar kids
Call him a greaser. I wish I could take an engine apart
        and reassemble it.
I also wish I sincerely wanted to. I don't. "Love is everything
        that it's
Cracked up to be." There's a song for you. Another is in the silence
Of a windless day. Hear it? Motors, yes, and the scrabbling
        of the surf
But, too, the silence in which out of the muck arise violet leaves
(Leaves of violets, that is). The days slide by and we feel we must
Stamp an impression on them. It is quite other. They
        stamp us, both
Time and season so that looking back there are wide
        unpeopled avenues
Blue-gray with cars on them, parked either side, and a
        small bridge that
Crosses Rock Creek has four bison at its corners, out of scale
Yet so mysterious to childhood, friendly, ominous, pattable because
Of bronze. The rain comes back, this spring, like a thirsty dog
Who goes back and back to his dish. "Fill it up, please," wag wag.

Gray depression and purple shadows, the daffodils feigning sunlight
That came yesterday. One day rain, one day sun,
    the weather is stuck
Like a record. Through it all the forsythia begins to bloom, brown
And yellow and warm as lit gas jets, clinging like bees to
The arching canes where starlings take cover from
    foraging cats. Not
To know: what have these years of living and being lived taught us?
Not to quarrel? Scarcely. You want to shoot pool, I
    want to go home:
And just before the snap of temper one had sensed so
Strongly the pleasure of watching a game well played: the cue ball
Carom and the struck ball pocketed. Skill. And still the untutored
Rain comes down. Open the laundry door. Press your face into the
Wet April chill: a life mask. Attune yourself to what is happening
Now, the little wet things, like washing up the lunch dishes.
    Bubbles
Rise, rinse and it is done. Let the dishes air-dry, the way
You let your hair after a shampoo. All evaporates, water,
    time, the
Happy moments and—harder to believe—the unhappy. Time on a
    bus,
That passes, and the night with its burthen and gift of dreams. That
Other life we live and need, filled with joys and terrors, threaded
By dailiness: where the wished-for sometimes happens, or, just
Before waking tremulous hands undo buttons. Another day, the sun
Comes out from behind unbuttoned cloud underclothes—gray
    with use—
And bud scales litter the sidewalks. A new shop is being built,
An old one refurbished. What was a white interior will
    now be brown
Behind men's clothes, there are these changes in taste. Fashion
It anew. Change in everything yet none so great as the changes in
Oneself, which, short of sickness, go unobserved. Why watch
Yourself? You know you're here, and where tomorrow you
    probably will

Be. In the delicatessen a woman made a fumbling gesture then
Slowly folded toward the floor. "Get a doctor,"
    someone said. "She's
Having a fit." Not knowing how to help I left, taking with me
The look of appeal in faded blue eyes. Between these sharp attacks
Of harsh reality I would like to interpose: interpose is not the
Word. One wants them not to happen, that's all,
    but, like slammed-
On brakes—the cab skids, you are thrown forward, ouch—they
Come. Times when religion would help: "Be merciful" "Intercede"
"That which I should have done . . ." Fear and
    superstition and some-
Thing more. But without the conviction of a truth, best leave
It alone. Life, it seems, explains nothing about itself. In the
Garden now daffodils stand full unfolded and
    to see them is enough.
They seem no more passing than when they weren't there: perhaps
The promise when first the blades pierced the wintry soil
Was better? You see, you invent choices where none exist. Perhaps
It is not a choice but a preference? No, take it all, it's free,
Help yourself. The sap rises. The trees leaf out and bloom. You
Suddenly sense: you don't know what. An exhilaration that revives
Old views and surges of energy or the pure pleasure of
Simply looking. A car goes over a rise and there are birches snow
Twisted into cabalistic shapes: The Devil's Notch; or Smuggler's
Gap. At the time you could not have imagined the time when you
Would forget the name, as apparent and there as your own. Rivers
Reflecting silver skies, how many boys have swum in you? A rope
Tied to a tree caught between my thighs and I was yanked headfirst
And fell into the muddy creek. What a long time it seemed, rising
To the surface, how lucky it didn't catch me in the groin. That
Won't happen twice, I imagine. That summer sun was the same
As this April one: is repetition boring? Or only inactivity? Quite
A few things are boring, like the broad avenues of Washington,
D.C., that seem to go from nowhere and back again. Civil servants
Wait at the crossing to cross to lunch at the Waffle House. In

This twilight Degas a woman sits and holds a fan, it's
The just rightness that counts. And how have you
        come to know just
Rightness when you see it and what is the deep stirring that it
Brings? Art is as mysterious as nature, as life, of which it is
A flower. Under the hedges now the weedy strips grow bright
With dandelions, just as good a flower as any other. Unfortunately,
You can't pick them: they wilt. But these burgeoning days are
Not like any others. Promise is a part of it, promise of warmth
And vegetative growth. "Wheel me out into the sun, Sonny,
These old bones that creak need it." And the gardener does not
Come back: over the winter he had a heart attack, has to take it
Easy. You see death shadowed out in another's life. The threat
Is always there, even in balmy April sunshine. So what
If it is hard to believe in? Stopping in the city while the light
Is red, to think that all who stop with you too must stop, and
Yet it is not less individual a fate for all that. "When I
was born, death kissed me. I kissed it back." Meantime, there
Is bridge, and solitaire, and phone calls and a door slams, someone
Goes out into the April sun to take a spin as far as the
Grocer's, to shop, and then come back. In the fullness of time,
Let me hand you an empty cup, coffee-stained. Or a small glass
Of spirits: "Here's your ounce of whisky for today." Next door
The boys dribble a basketball and practice shots. Two boys
Run by: high spirits. The postman comes. No mail of interest.
Another day, there is. A postcard of the Washington Monument,
A friend waving from a small window at the needle top. "Hoo
Hoo" he calls. Another day, and still the sun shines down, warming
Tulips into bloom, a redder red than blood. The dandelions
Cringe before them. In the evening there will be time enough
To drive from here to there, study the vegetable patch, admire
The rosy violets. Life in action, life in repose, life in
Contemplation, which is hard to tell from daydreaming, on a day
When the sky woolgathers clouds and sets their semblance on a
Glassy ocean. Only its edge goes lisp. On no two days the same.
Is it the ocean's mindlessness that troubles? At times it seems
Calculatedly malevolent, tearing the dunes asunder, tumbling

Summer houses into itself, a terror to see. They say there are
Those who have never felt terror. A slight creeping of the scalp,
Merely. How fine. Finer than sand, that, on a day like this,
Trickles through my fingers, ensconced in a dune cleft, sun-
Warmed and breeze-cooled. This peace is full of sounds and
Movement. A couple passes, jogging. A dog passes, barking
And running. My nose runs, a little. Just a drip. Left over
From winter. How long ago it seems! All spring and summer stretch
Ahead, a roadway lined by roses and thunder. "It will be here
Before you know it." These twigs will then have leafed and
Shower down a harvest of yellow-brown. So far away, so
Near at hand. The sand runs through my fingers. The yellow
Daffodils have white corollas (sepals?). The crocuses are gone,
I didn't see them go. They were here, now they're not. Instead
The forsythia ensnarls its flames, cool fire, pendent
        above the smoke
Of its brown branches. Beaches are near. It rains again: the screen
And window glass are pebbled by it. It soaks through
        a raincoat that
Has had its water repellency dry-cleaned out of it. Most modern
Inventions don't work so well, or not for long. A breakdown occurs,
Or something simple, like the dishwasher detergent eating off
The pattern on china, even the etched florets on wineglasses.
Strong stuff. From the train, a stand of larch is greener than
Greenest grass. A funny tree, of many moods, gold in autumn,
        naked
In winter: an evergreen (it looks) that isn't. What kind of a tree
Is that? I love to see it resurrect itself, the enfolded buttons
Of needles studding the branches, then opening into little bursts.
And that Washington flower, the pink magnolia tree, blooms now
In little yards, its trunk a smoky gray. And soon the hybrid azaleas,
So much too much, will follow, and the tender lilac. Persia, we
Have much to thank you for, besides the word lapis lazuli. And
        someone
You know well is suffering, sees it all but not the way before
Him, hating his job and not knowing what to change it for. Have
You any advice to give? Have you learned nothing in all these

Years? "Take it as it comes." Sit still and listen: each so alone.
Someone driving decides not to take that curve, to pile it up
In smithereens, the anxious and unsatisfying years: goodbye, life.
Others keep on living so as not to wound their friends: the suicide
Fantasy, to awaken rested and fresh, to plunge into a deep and
Dreamless sleep, to be mindless and at one with all that grows,
Dies and revives each April, here, crying, "Stir your stumps!"
In the mental hospital a patient is ready to be discharged. "I'm
So glad to be going home!" Where the same old problems wait;
Still, to feel more equal to them, that's something. "Time heals
All wounds": now what's that supposed to mean? Wounds can
Kill, like that horse-chestnut tree with the rotting place will surely
Die unless the tree doctor comes. Cut out the rot, fill with tree
Cement, score and leave to heal. The rain comes down in buckets:
I've never seen that, though you often speak of it. The rain
Comes down and brings depression, too much and too often. And
    there
Is the fog off the cold Atlantic. No one is at his best with
A sinus headache. It will pass. Stopped passages unblock: why
Let the lovely spring, its muck and scarlet emperors, get you
Down. Unhibernate. Let the rain soak your hair, run down your
Face, hang in drops from facial protuberances. Face into
It, then towel dry. Then another day brings back the sun and
Violets in the grass. The pear tree thickens all its boughs and
Twigs into silver-white, a dimmed brilliance, and already at
Its base a circle of petals on the unmowed grass. Far away
In Washington, at the Reflecting Pool, the Japanese cherries
Bust out into their dog mouth pink. Visitors gasp. The sun
Drips, coats and smears, all that spring yellow under unending
Blue. Only the oaks hold back their leaf buds, reticent.
Reticence is not a bad quality, though it may lead to
    misunderstandings.
I misunderstood silence for disapproval, see now it was
Sympathy. Thank you, May, for these warm stirrings. Life
Goes on, it seems, though in all sorts of places—nursing
Homes—it is drawing to a close. Abstractions and generalities:
Grass and blue depths into which the evening star seems set.

As windows are set in walls in whited Washington. City, begone
From my thoughts: childhood was not all that gay. Nor all that
    gray,
For the matter of that. May leans in my window, offering hornets.
To them too I give leave to go about their business, which is not
Nesting in my books. The fresh-mown lawn is a rug underneath
Which is swept the dirt, the living dirt out of which our nurture
Comes, to which we go, not knowing if we hasten or we tarry. May
Opens wide her bluest eyes and speaks in bird tongues and a
Chain saw. The blighted elms come down. Already maple saplings,
Where elms once grew and whelmed, count as young trees. In
A dishpan the soap powder dissolves under a turned-on faucet and
Makes foam, like the waves that crash ashore at the foot
Of the street. A restless surface. Chewing, and spitting sand and
Small white pebbles, clam shells with a sheen or chalky white.
A horseshoe crab: primeval. And all this without thought, this
Churning energy. Energy! The sun sucks up the dew; the day is
Clear; a bird shits on my window ledge. Rain will wash it off
Or a storm will chip it loose. Life, I do not understand.
Days tick by, each so unique, each so alike: what is that chatter
In the grass? May is not a flowering month so much as shades
Of green, yellow-green, blue-green, or emerald or dusted like
The lilac leaves. The lilac trusses stand in bud. A cardinal
Passes like a flying tulip, alights and nails the green day
Down. One flame in a fire of sea-soaked, copper-fed wood:
A red that leaps from green and holds it there. Reluctantly
The plane tree, always late, as though from age, opens up and
Hangs its seed balls out. The apples flower. The pear is past.
Winter is suddenly so far away, behind, ahead. From the train
A stand of coarse grass in fuzzy flower. Is it for miracles
We live? I love it when the morning sun lights up my room
Like a yellow jelly bean, an inner glow. May mutters, "Why
ask questions?" or, "What are the questions you wish to ask?"

The Morning of
the Poem

[1 9 8 0]

This Dark Apartment

Coming from the deli
a block away today I
saw the UN building
shine and in all the
months and years I've
lived in this apartment
I took so you and I
would have a place to
meet I never noticed
that it was in my view.

I remember very well
the morning I walked in
and found you in bed
with X. He dressed
and left. You dressed
too. I said, "Stay
five minutes." You
did. You said, "That's
the way it is." It
was not much of a surprise.

Then X got on speed
and ripped off an
antique chest and an
air conditioner, etc.
After he was gone and
you had changed the
Segal lock, I asked
you on the phone, "Can't
you be content with
your wife and me?" "I'm
not built that way,"
you said. No surprise.

Now, without saying
why, you've let me go.
You don't return my
calls, who used to call
me almost every evening
when I lived in the coun-
try. "Hasn't he told you
why?" "No, and I doubt he
ever will." Goodbye. It's
mysterious and frustrating.

How I wish you would come
back! I could tell
you how, when I lived
on East 49th, first
with Frank and then with John,
we had a lovely view of
the UN building and the
Beekman Towers. They were
not my lovers, though.
You were. You said so.

June 30, 1974

For Jane and Joe Hazan

Let me tell you
that this weekend Sunday
morning in the country
fills my soul
with tranquil joy:
the dunes beyond
the pond beyond
the humps of bayberry—
my favorite
shrub (today,
at least)—are
silent as a mountain
range: such a
subtle profile
against a sky that
goes from dawn
to blue. The roses
stir, the grapevine
at one end of the deck
shakes and turns
its youngest leaves
so they show pale
and flower-like.
A redwing blackbird
pecks at the grass;
another perches on a bush.
Another way, a millionaire's
white château turns
its flank to catch
the risen sun. No
other houses, except
this charming one,
alive with paintings,

163

plants and quiet.
I haven't said
a word. I like
to be alone
with friends. To get up
to this morning view
and eat poached eggs
and extra toast with
Tiptree Gooseberry Preserve
(green)—and coffee,
milk, no sugar. Jane
said she heard
the freeze-dried kind
is healthier when
we went shopping
yesterday and she
and John bought
crude blue Persian plates.
How can coffee be
healthful? I mused
as sunny wind
streamed in the car
window driving home.
Home! How lucky to
have one, how arduous
to make this scene
of beauty for
your family and
friends. Friends!
How we must have
sounded, gossiping at
the dinner table
last night. Why, *that*
dinner table is
this breakfast table:
"The boy in trousers
is not the same boy

in no trousers," who
said? Discontinuity
in all we see and are:
the same, yet change,
change, change. "Inez,
it's good to see you."
Here comes the cat, sedate,
that killed and brought
a goldfinch yesterday.
I'd like to go out
for a swim but
it's a little cool
for that. Enough to
sit here drinking coffee,
writing, watching the clear
day ripen (such
a rainy June we had)
while Jane and Joe
sleep in their room
and John in his. I
think I'll make more toast.

Korean Mums

beside me in this garden
are huge and daisy-like
(why not? are not
oxeye daisies a chrysanthemum?),
shrubby and thick-stalked,
the leaves pointing up
the stems from which
the flowers burst in
sunbursts. I love
this garden in all its moods,
even under its winter coat
of salt hay, or now,
in October, more than
half gone over: here
a rose, there a clump
of aconite. This morning
one of the dogs killed
a barn owl. Bob saw
it happen, tried to
intervene. The airedale
snapped its neck and left
it lying. Now the bird
lies buried by an apple
tree. Last evening
from the table we saw
the owl, huge in the dusk,
circling the field
on owl-silent wings.
The first one ever seen
here: now it's gone,
a dream you just remember.

The dogs are barking. In
the studio music plays

and Bob and Darragh paint.
I sit scribbling in a little
notebook at a garden table,
too hot in a heavy shirt
in the mid-October sun
into which the Korean mums
all face. There is a
dull book with me,
an apple core, cigarettes,
an ashtray. Behind me
the rue I gave Bob
flourishes. Light on leaves,
so much to see, and
all I really see is that
owl, its bulk troubling
the twilight. I'll
soon forget it: what
is there I have not forgot?
Or one day will forget:
this garden, the breeze
in stillness, even
the words, Korean mums.

Song

The light lies layered in the leaves.
Trees, and trees, more trees.
A cloud boy brings the evening paper:
The Evening Sun. It sets.
Not sharply or at once
a stately progress down the sky
(it's gilt and pink and faintly green)
above, beyond, behind the evening leaves
of trees. Traffic sounds and
bells resound in silver clangs
the hour, a tune, my friend
Pierrot. The violet hour:
the grass is violent green.
A weeping beech is gray,
a copper beech is copper red.
Tennis nets hang
unused in unused stillness.
A car starts up and
whispers into what will soon be night.
A tennis ball is served.
A horsefly vanishes.
A smoking cigarette.
A day (so many and so few)
dies down a hardened sky
and leaves are lap-held notebook leaves
discriminated barely
in light no longer layered.

Wystan Auden

I went to his fortieth birthday
party: was it really twenty-seven
years ago? I don't remember what
street he was living on, but he
was adapting *The Duchess of Malfi*:
Canada Lee appeared in white face:
it was that long ago. It was in
that apartment I just missed
meeting Brecht and T. S. Eliot.

I remember Chester so often saying,
"Oh *Wystan!*" while Wystan looked
pleased at having stirred him up.

On Ischia he claimed to take
St. Restituta seriously, and
sat at Maria's café in the cobbled
square saying, "Poets should
dress like businessmen," while
he wore an incredible peach-
colored nylon shirt. And on
Fire Island his telling someone,
"You must write each book as
though it were your last." And
when he learned that in Florence
I and my friend Bill Aalto had
fished his drafts of poems
out of the wastepaper basket,
he took to burning them, saying,
"I feel like an ambassador burning
secret papers." When he got off
the liner at Naples, in black and
a homburg, he said, "I've just
read *all* of Doughty's *The Dawn*

in Britain." And earlier, right
after the war, "My dear, I'm the
first major poet to have flown
the Atlantic." He was very kind.
Once, when I had an operation
in Rome, he wrote me quite a large
check: I forget for how much.
When I sent it back and asked
for (for a more favorable ex-
change on the black market)
cash, he sent it, along with
a cross note saying he was
a busy man. Once when a group
of us made an excursion from
Ischia—Capri, Sorrento, Positano,
Amalfi, Pompeii—he suddenly
said at cocktails on a pensione
terrace: "More of this sitting
around like beasts!" He was
industrious, writing away in
a smoky room—fug—in a
ledger or on loose sheets
poems, some of which I typed
for him (they're in *Nones*).

I don't have to burn his
letters as he asked his
friends to do: they were lost
a long time ago. So much
to remember, so little to
say: that he liked martinis
and was greedy about the wine?
I always thought he would live
to a great age. He did not.
Wystan, kind man, great poet,
goodbye.

Dining Out with Doug and Frank

For Frank Polach

Not quite yet. First,
around the corner for a visit
to the Bella Landauer Collection
of printed ephemera:
luscious lithos and why did
Fairy Soap vanish and
Crouch and Fitzgerald survive?
Fairy Soap was once a
household word! I've been living
at Broadway and West 74th
for a week and still haven't
ventured on a stroll in
Central Park, two bizarre blocks
away. (Bizarre is for the ex-
town houses, mixing Byzantine
with Gothic and Queen Anne.)
My abstention from the park
is for Billy Nichols who went
bird-watching there and, for
his binoculars, got his
head beat in. Streaming blood,
he made it to an avenue
where no cab would pick him up
until one did and at
Roosevelt Hospital he waited
several hours before any
doctor took him in hand. A
year later he was dead. But
I'll make the park: I carry
more cash than I should and
walk the street at night
without feeling scared unless
someone scary passes.

Now it's tomorrow,
as usual. Turned out that
Doug (Douglas Crase, the poet)
had to work (he makes his bread
writing speeches): thirty pages
explaining why Eastman Kodak's
semi-slump (?) is just what
the stockholders ordered. He
looked glum, and declined
a drink. By the by did you know
that John Ashbery's grandfather
was offered an investment-in
when George Eastman founded his
great corporation? He turned it
down. Eastman Kodak will survive.
"Yes" and where would our
John be now? I can't imagine him
any different than he is,
a problem which does not arise,
so I went with Frank (the poet,
he makes his dough as a librarian,
botanical librarian at Rutgers
and as a worker he's a beaver:
up at 5:30, home after 7, but
over striped bass he said he
had begun to see the unwisdom
of his ways and next week will
revert to the seven-hour day
for which he's paid. Good. Time
and energy to write. Poetry
takes it out of you, or you
have to have a surge to bring
to it. Words. So useful and
pleasant) to dine at McFeely's
at West 23rd and Eleventh Avenue
by the West River, which is

the right name for the Hudson
when it bifurcates from
the East River to create
Manhattan "an isle of joy."
Take my word for it, don't
(shall I tell you about my
friend who effectively threw
himself under a train in
the Times Square station?
No. Too tender to touch. In
fact, at the moment I've blocked
out his name. No I haven't:
Peter Kemeny, gifted and tormented
fat man) listen to anyone
else.

III

Oh. At the Battery all
that water becomes the
North River, which seems
to me to make no sense
at all. I always thought
Castle Garden faced Calais.

IV

Peconic Bay scallops, the
tiny, the real ones and cooked
in butter, not breaded and
plunged in deep grease. The food
is good and reasonable (for these
days) but the point is McFeely's
itself—the owner's name or
was it always called that? It's
the bar of the old Terminal Hotel
and someone (McFeely?) has had
the wit to restore it to what

it was: all was there, under
layers of paint and abuse, neglect.
You, perhaps, could put a date
on it: I'll vote for 1881
or the 70's. The ceiling is
florid glass, like the cabbage-rose
runners in the grand hotels
at Saratoga: when were they built?
The bar is thick and long and
sinuous, virile. Mirrors: are
the decorations on them cut
or etched? I do remember that
above the men's room door the
word Toilet is etched
on a transom. Beautiful lettering,
but nothing to what lurks
within: the three most
splendid urinals I've ever
seen. Like Roman steles. I
don't know what I was going
to say. Yes. Does the Terminal Hotel
itself still function? (Did you
know that "they" sold all the
old mirror glass out of Gage
and Tollner's? Donald Droll has
a fit every time he eats there.)
"Terminal," I surmise, because
the hotel faced the terminal
of the 23rd Street ferry, a
perfect sunset sail to Hoboken
and the yummies of the Clam
Broth House, which, thank God,
still survives. Not many do:
Gage and Tollner's, the Clam Broth House,
McSorley's and now McFeely's. Was
that the most beautiful of the
ferry houses or am I thinking
of Christopher Street? And there

was another uptown that crossed
to Jersey and back but docking
further downtown: it sailed
on two diagonals. And wasn't
there one at 42nd? It couldn't
matter less, they're gone, all
gone and we are left with just
the Staten Island ferry, all
right in its way but how often
do you want to pass Miss Liberty
and see that awesome spiky postcard
view? The river ferryboats were
squat and low like tugs, old
and wooden and handsome, you
were *in* the water, *in* the shipping:
Millay wrote a poem about
it all. I cannot accept their
death, or any other death. Bill
Aalto, my first lover (five tumultuous
years found Bill chasing me around
the kitchen table—in Wystan Auden's
house in Forio d'Ischia—with
a carving knife. He was serious
and so was I and so I wouldn't go
when he wanted to see me when
he was dying of leukemia. Am I
sorry? Not really. The fear had
gone too deep. The last time I
saw him was in the City Center lobby
and he was jolly—if he just
stared at you and the tears began
it was time to cut and run—
and the cancer had made him lose
a lot of weight and he looked
young and handsome as the night
we picked each other up
in Pop Tunick's long-gone gay bar.
Bill never let me forget that

on the jukebox I kept playing
Lena Horne's "Mad about the Boy."
Why the nagging teasing? It's
a great performance but he
thought it was East Fifties queen
taste. Funny—or, funnily enough—
in dreams, and I dream about him
a lot, he's always the nice guy
I first knew and loved, not
the figure of terror he became.
Oh well. Bill had his hour: he
was a hero, a major in the
Abraham Lincoln Brigade. A dark
Finn who looked not unlike
a butch version of Valentino.
Watch out for Finns. They're
murder when they drink) used
to ride the ferries all the
time, doing the bars along
the waterfront: did you know
Hoboken has—or had—
more bars (Death.
At least twice when
someone I knew and hated
died I felt the joy of vengeance:
I mean I smiled and laughed out
loud: a hateful feeling.
It passes) to the square inch
than any other city? "Trivia,
Goddess . . ." Through dinner
I wanted to talk more than we
did about Frank's poems. All it
came down to was "experiment
more," "try collages," and "write
some skinny poems" but I like
where he's heading now and
Creative Writing has never

been my trip although I understand
the fun of teaching someone
something fun to do although most people
simply have not got the gift
and where's the point? What
puzzles me is what my friends
find to say. Oh, forget it. Reading,
writing, knowing other poets
will do it, if there is
anything doing. The reams
of shit I've read. It would
have been so nice after dinner
to take a ferry boat with Frank
across the Hudson (or West River,
if you prefer). To be on
the water in the dark and
the wonder of electricity—
the real beauty of Manhattan.
Oh well. When they tore down
the Singer Building,
and when I saw the Bogardus Building
rusty and coming unstitched in
a battlefield of rubble I deliberately
withdrew my emotional investments
in loving old New York. Except
you can't. I really like
dining out and last night was
especially fine. A full moon
when we parted hung over
Frank and me. Why is this poem
so long? And full of death?
Frank and Doug are young and
beautiful and have nothing
to do with that. Why is this poem
so long? "Enough is as good
as a feast" and I'm a Herrick fan.
I'd like to take that plunge

into Central Park, only I'm
waiting for Darragh Park to phone.
Oh. Doug and Frank. One is light,
the other dark.
Doug is the tall one.

The Payne Whitney Poems

written in while in an institution

Trip

Wigging in, wigging out:
when I stop to think
the wires in my head
cross: kaboom. How
many trips
by ambulance (five,
count them five),
claustrated, pill addiction,
in and out of mental
hospitals,
the suicidalness (once
I almost made it)
but—I go on?
Tell you all of it?
I can't. When I think
of that, that at
only fifty-one I,
Jim the Jerk, am
still alive and breathing
deeply, that I think
is a miracle.

We Walk

in the garden. Sun
on the river
flashing past. I
dig ivy leaves.
We walk in a
maze. Sun, shine
on. Now it is

179

one hour later.
Out the window no
sun. Cloud
turbulence and
the wind whistles.
Curious.

Arches

of buildings, this building,
frame a stream of windows
framed in white brick. This
building is fireproof; or else
it isn't: the furnishings first
to go: no, the patients. Patients
on Sundays walk in a small garden.
Today some go out on a group
pass. To stroll the streets and shop.
So what else is new? The sky
slowly/swiftly went blue to gray.
A gray in which some smoke stands.

Linen

Is this the moment?
No, not yet.
When is the
moment?
Perhaps there is
none.
Need I persist?

This morning I
changed bedding.
At lunch I watched
someone shake out

the tablecloth, fold
and stow it in a side-
board. Then, the
cigarette moment.
Now, this moment
flows out of me
down the pen and
writes.

I'm glad I have
fresh linen.

Heather and Calendulas

A violet hush: and sunbursts.
An aluminum measure
full of water. Scentlessness.
"Go to church next week?"
Fortuitous as nuts too
salty. Accordion pleats.
The phone bill is buff.
Three postcards of three
paintings. A good review.
Pale green walls and
a white ceiling. Lamps
lit in daylight. Ice.
The temperature 16. In
February. "Laugh and
the world laughs with you."
Die, and you die alone.

Back

from the Frick. The weather
cruel as Henry Clay himself.
Who put that collection together?

Duveen? I forget. It was nice
to see the masterpieces again,
covered with the strikers' blood.
What's with art anyway, that
we give it such precedence?
I love the paintings, that's for sure.
What I really loved today
was New York, its streets and
men selling flowers and hot dogs,
mysterious town houses,
the gritty wind. I used to live
around here but it's changed some.
Why? That was only thirty years ago.

Blizzard

Tearing and tearing
ripped-up bits of paper,
no, it's not paper
it's snow. Blown side-
ways in the wind,
coming in my window
wetting stacked books.
"Mr Park called. He
can't come visiting
today." Of course not,
in this driving icy
weather. How I wish
I were out in it! A
figure like an ex-
clamation point seen
through driving snow.

February 13, 1975

Tomorrow is St Valentine's:
tomorrow I'll think about
that. Always nervous, even
after a good sleep I'd like
to climb back into. The sun
shines on yesterday's new-
fallen snow and yestereven
it turned the world to pink
and rose and steel-blue
buildings. Helene is restless:
leaving soon. And what then
will I do with myself? Some-
one is watching morning
TV. I'm not reduced to that
yet. I wish one could press
snowflakes in a book like flowers.

Sleep

The friends who come to see you
and the friends who don't.
The weather in the window.
A pierced ear.
The mounting tension and the spasm.
A paper-lace doily on a small plate.
Tangerines.
A day in February: heart-
shaped cookies on St Valentine's.
Like Christopher, a discarded saint.
A tough woman with black hair.
"I got to set my wig straight."
A gold and silver day begins to wane.
A crescent moon.
Ice on the window.
Give my love to, oh, anybody.

Pastime

I pick up a loaded pen and twiddle it.
After the blizzard
cold days of shrinking snow.
At visiting hour the cars
below my window form up
in a traffic jam. A fast-
moving man is in charge,
herding the big machines
like cattle. Weirdly, it all
keeps moving somehow. I read
a dumb detective story. I
clip my nails: hard
as iron or glass. The clippers
keep sliding off them. Today
I'm shaky. A shave, a bath.
Chat. The morning paper.
Sitting. Staring. Thinking blankly.
TV. A desert kind of life.

What

What's in those pills?
After lunch and I can
hardly keep my eyes
open. Oh, for someone
to
talk small talk with.
Even a dog would do.

Why are they hammering
iron outside? And what
is that generator whose
fierce hum comes in

the window? What is a
poem, anyway.

The daffodils, the heather
and the freesias all
speak to me, I speak
back, like St Francis
and the wolf of Gubbio.

The Morning of the Poem

For Darragh Park

July 8 or July 9, the eighth surely, certainly
    1976 that I know
Awakening in western New York blurred barely
    morning sopping dawn
Globules face to my face, a beautiful face, not
    mine: Baudelaire's skull:
Force, fate, will, and, you being you: a
    painter, you drink
Your Ovaltine and climb to the city roof, "to
    find a view," and
I being whoever I am get out of bed holding
    my cock and go to piss
Then to the kitchen to make coffee and toast
    with jam and see out
The window two blue jays ripping something white
    while from my mother's
Room the radio purls: it plays all night she leaves
    it on to hear
The midnight news then sleeps and dozes
    until day which now it is,
Wakening today in green more gray, why did
    your lithe blondness
In Remsen handsomeness mix in my mind with
    Baudelaire's skull? which
Stands for strength and fierceness, the dedication
    of the artist?
How easily I could be in love with you,
    who do not like to be touched,
And yet I do not want to be in love with you,
    nor you with me,
"Strange business" the chinky Chinaman said and
    from the kitchen window
The jays are fatter than any jays I ever saw

before and hanging
In a parlor floor in far-off Chelsea I'm
    glad there is a
Watercolor of me in blue shorts, sitting
    beside a black *Britannica*
And a green-glass-shaded student lamp and
    a glass of deep red wine
Ruby wine the throat of a hummingbird
    hanging on speeding
Wings in fierce blue delphinium depths I think
About those two blue jays, like me, too
    chubby, and Baudelaire's skull,
That sees in the tattered morning the passing of
The lost and indigent, the lost, the way
    the day when I arose
Seemed lost and trash-picking for a meatless morsel,
    a stinking
Bone, such as in this green unlovely village
    one need never
Seek or fear and you descend to your studio
    leaving on your roof
The exhalation of Baudelaire's image of
    terror which is
Not terror but the artist's (your) determination
    to be strong
To see things as they are too fierce and yet
    not too much: in
Western New York, why Baudelaire? In Chelsea,
    why not? Smile,
July day. Why did Baudelaire wander in? Don't
    I love Heine more? Or
Walt Whitman, Walt? No, they come to my death-
    bed and one by one take my hand
And say, "So long, old man," and who was it
    who in the Café Montana told,
In all seriousness, that the triumph of Mrs S.,
    future Duchess of W., was that

"They say she's a circus in bed." I like to
      dwell on that, the caged lions
And the whips, ball-balancing seals, "And now,
      without a net . . ." the odious
Clowns: boring Ensor and pseudo-symbolism of
      something meaning something
That doesn't mean a thing at all: the simplicity
      of true drama, a trained and
Modulated voice, a hand that rises of itself.
      "La commedia non par finita;
Ma pure è finita" pleasant to be
      Goldoni and meet Mr Tiepolo in
The square, or Longhi, Guardi, or am I mixing
      up my dates: somebody was older
Than somebody and Goldoni went off to France
      on another gray morning in
Which the firs crowd too thickly on these village
      lawns: Chestnut Hill Road,
But the blight came and there are no chestnuts;
      the blight came, and there
Are no elms; only spruce and maples, maple saplings
      springing up in hedges,
A skinny weed, and this weed, this wild yellow
      flower lower and larger than
A buttercup, not lacquer yellow, more the yellow
      of a marsh marigold, meaty
Like it, though not so large, not nearly so
      large, sprinkled in the weedy
Wild-flower lawn, for God's sake, what is your
      name? "Will you have the watermelon
And the iced coffee, dear?" "Comrades, leave me
      read my *Times.*" She sets
The dishes out just so, as though to please me
      and to please her, a right
Way to do things and that is how she does them. The watermelon
      is fresh
And good and behind this grunt of words I see

188

you, Baudelaire's mask your sign,
Legs apart, addressed to your easel, squeezing
    out the tubes of oils
Whose names you know: what is that green you
    use so much of, that seems to
Devour itself? Nor can I quite forget what someone
    said: "I got her number:
'Why did you tell him homosexuality is a neurosis?' "
    I said, "She said
She didn't say it, but she did." Hard to
    achieve with so much information
Available, so little to be believed. Last July
    was an inferno, tempests of
Rain, then seared grass, this July overcast
    with hottish afternoons: I
Begrudge that far-off island in Penobscot Bay,
    mossy walks and Twin Flower
Corner, icy swims in early morning off pebble
    beaches, the smell of juniper
Where my dead best friend will always walk
    beside me, stride ahead of me.
"When I walk with you, all I see is the heels
    of your sneakers": were
You buried in your sneakers? Of course not,
    though in a tender joke you were:
A nosegay tossed on the coffin: but this is not
    your poem, your poem I may
Never write, too much, though it is there and
    needs only to be written down
And one day will and if it isn't it doesn't matter:
    the truth, the absolute
Of feeling, of knowing what you know, that is
    the poem, like
The house for sale buried in a luxuriance of
    overgrown foundation planting
Across the street upon this hill (taxus,
    cotoneaster), the doctor has more

189

Patients in Buffalo: he moved there: I'd rather
        stay here and starve, well,
Sort of starve: yesterday I tripped on a scatter
        rug and slam fell full length,
The wind knocked out of me: "Shall I call a
        doctor?" "Please don't talk"
"Are you hurt? Can I help you?" "Shut the fuck
        up" I thought I'd smashed
My kneecap—you know, like when you really
        wham your funny bone, only
More so—but I got up and felt its nothing-
        broken-tenderness and
Hobbled down this everlasting hill to distant
        Bell's and bought
Edible necessities: small icy cans of concentrated
        juice, lemon, lime, orange,
Vast puffy bags of bread, Smucker's raspberry jam,
        oatmeal, but not the good,
The Irish kind (travel note: in New York City you
        almost cannot buy a bowl
Of oatmeal: I know, I've tried: why bother: it
        would only taste like paste)
And hobbled home, studying the for-sale house
        hidden in scaly leaves
The way the brownstone facing of your house is
        coming off in giant flakes: there's
A word for that sickness of the stone but I
        can't remember it (you'll find
It in that fascinating book *Brick and Brownstone*:
        illustrative photograph)
And in July you take a picture in progress out,
        your street in snow,
Air conditioners capped with snow and in the
        distance the problem,
An office building straight from Babylon: a
        friend said of you, "With people,
He's awfully good," meaning, I surmise, "kind,

considerate," "Oh," I said,
"When he has to, he can put his foot down," "I'm
    very glad," our friend
Said, "to hear *that*." Not that he or I meant
    you have a taint
Of toughness, just, well, time passes and
    sometimes you must say "No"
Or, "Don't tread on me" but don't change, I
    like you as you are, laughing
So loud in Sagaponack the summer neighbors
    sent the maid to poke through
Privet and say "There's too much noise": we were
    stunned: complaints about
Laughing? We go on, but, of course, it's not
    quite the same under
An almost autumn sky, a swimming pool awash
    with cinnamon and gentian
(The sky's the swimming pool, that is) why is
    each day dawning so alike? Overcast,
Or gray: choose one: and then there was the just-
    before-morning electric storm
Night before last: two killed by bolt in a
    Batavia park: my room lighting up
Bright enough to read by. "Fear no more the heat
    of the sun, nor the all-
Dreaded thunder-stone," funny, lightning doesn't
    scare me any more, it thrills,
So long as I'm indoors, in bed by preference,
    with pillows under which to tuck
My head against the louder claps. I'm very brave.
    Then a shovelful of earth
Is thrown into the open grave and rattles on
    the coffin. Oh goodbye, goodbye.
I want to go away into that blue or dark or
    certain or uncertain land: why
Can't we know that it is there and there we'll
    meet and grow in friendship

As we have here? You know that Austrian operetta,
    don't you, *The Land of Smiles*?
That is not what I mean. I'm often happiest
    walking crosstown on a bright
And icy day when up above mare's-tails sparkle and
    I stop to inspect the junk
In junk-shop windows and pass on feasting my eyes
    on what to me is beefy
Handsomeness, sexiness, I don't want it really,
    just to recollect or think,
My, that's nice, warm flesh on a cold, cold
    day: today, July, country edge,
There's almost a chill, and the knee I fell on
    throbs more than
Yesterday. What a drag. Michael Lally is a fine
    poet and looks straight
Into your eyes. I know someone else who looks
    deep into your eyes and under
The curly hair the lies are manufactured. Mostly,
    it delights me, like
A farce, the need to dramatize, to make out, "Oh
    I was beautiful, oh the most
Famous men all fell for me and slipped it up
    my cooze. I've seen
'em all!" I believe you, dear. More kinds of
    conifers than spruce grow
On this hill. I wish I knew their names, I have
    a friend, a botanist,
Who could tell them to me, one by one. Frank lives
    in London Terrace and this
Is the London Terrace story. There's something
    called the Poison Line:
When someone, children mostly, goes, say, munching
    in the woods and gets sick
The doctors set the phone wires flashing to
    hospitals, horticultural
Gardens, informed New York. It was 3 a.m., my

192

friend was asleep in
    London Terrace. The phone. Off in Virginia a young
        man had quarreled
With his family so he went out in the yard and
        gathered castor beans.
They have a hard shell and if you swallow them
        like that they pass
Harmlessly through. He crushed them first.
        Eight is a lethal dose. He
Picked ten. A young man in Virginia. "What happened?"
        "I said, induce
Vomiting. I'm sure it was too late." "Did he die?"
        "I don't know: I
Tried to check back but I couldn't make contact."
        And all that castor
Oil they used to pour down me when I was a kid!
        Pity the young Virginian.
And still it's chill and overcast and in the afternoon
        we went next door
To tea: a house I'd lived next door to for
        forty years and never been inside
Of, not once, before. Mrs Blank, the dead, the former
        owner, wasn't much for
Entertaining high-school boys. She died mad, her
        little hands clenched in
Monkey fists and wouldn't eat her food. Her husband,
        the arborist, he's
Gone too, and handsome Larry, crushed by a car
        against the back wall of a garage:
Die, die, die, and only pray the pain won't be more
        than you can bear. But
What you must bear, you will. I've known a
        murderer (or two): or were
They only bragging? Not everyone is quite so nice
        as my gentle Grandma Ella
Sleeping away off there in Albert Lea, Minnesota,
        where even the lake

Is named Lake Albert Lea: who was he? A surveyor,
    it seems to me: you can
See the lake in this snapshot of my mother, kneeling
    on the lawn, using
Her turned-over hat to hold a big bunch of sweet
    William: stop stirring
The rice and come with me to Maine and we'll settle
    once for all which
Is woundwort and which Jill-over-the-ground: but
    you're painting, or sketching
In big charcoal strokes what will become a painting:
    I'm posing, seated
By the tall window and the Ming tree, and look
    out across the Chelsea street
And up to where a handsome muscular man in just
    a towel leans out into
The snow (it isn't always July, you know) to see
    what's going on: my heart
Goes pitta-pat, but you, you won't even down
    your brush and take a peek:
I call that dedication: painting, stirring rice,
    scooting off
To see the great Arletty as Garance: busy, busy:
    happy, happy? Sometimes
I think so, surely hope so: perhaps what I mean
    is happier, happier,
Plunged in work, sorting out your head: "*Bonjour,
madame, I* am little
Marcel Proust" "I take the subway, then the cross-
    town bus, the small Rembrandt
On the wall," that's rather grand, you know, however
    small, and to the collection
Now is added one by you and that too is pleasing
    and not ungrand: July
Days pass, the brushes slide and pull the paint:
    out your window
Do the roses bloom? I hope so: how I love roses!

Bunches of roses on
The dining table, Georg Arends, big and silver-
        pink with sharply
Bent-back petals so the petals make a point.
Or Variegata di Bologna, streaked and freaked
        in raspberries and cream,
A few gathered into an amethyst wineglass:
        nothing like it and I
Love them, not over yet early in July, this cold
        July, the grass for once
Is not overmown, burnt off: the mower is set too
        close, it frustrates
Me. Typing in my undershorts, I'm cold; abroad,
        England, France,
Denmark, Germany (oh yes, and Italy), they've had
        a four-week heat wave and
A drought. The pastures for the cows are all
        burnt off, only the grapes
In France are happy, what a bonanza there will
        be, wine, rich and grapy,
No treat, alas, for those who don't imbibe: rich
        as those Poiret robes
And dresses I went to see in the cellar of the
        Fashion Institute:
A brown that isn't purple, gamboge, celadon lined
        with jade, fat fur cuffs,
Turbans stuck with black aigrettes, luxury and
        wit: tell me, you who know,
What is that bird big as a duck that's not a
        duck on the grass with a black
Bib and dark tan stripes, is it a kind of dove
        or pigeon? What would I gain
By knowing? Like West 20th Street, West 22nd
        Street, a white high rise at
Number 360 where the International Supermarket
        nestles? And the Seminary
Enclosing a court of grass and trees, dark-

green-smelling cut-out shapes on
The evening we took our stroll there. Nearby,
    the sadomasochistic bars
With men in nails and boots and leather and
    the heavier sort of denim,
Clanking keys, the risky docks: you'd be
    well advised to keep
Away from: a lot of it of course is
    just for show (children playing
Dress-ups) but some of it is more, how you say,
    for real: I saw a man's
Back where someone had played tick-tack-toe
    with a knife. His wife has
Left him. "Have some speed: makes you feel
    real sexy," get away from me you
Poet with no talent, only a gift to destroy:
    when our best poet was invited
To review one of your little offerings I said,
    "Won't it be like
Reviewing your reflection in an oil slick?"
    So many lousy poets
    So few good ones
    What's the problem?
    No innate love of
    Words, no sense of
    How the thing said
    Is in the words, how
    The words are themselves
    The thing said: love,
    Mistake, promise, auto
    Crack-up, color, petal,
    The color in the petal
    Is merely light
    And that's refraction:
    A word, that's the poem.
    A blackish-red nasturtium.
    Roses shed on

A kitchen floor, a
Cool and scented bed
To loll and roll on.
I wish I had a rose
Or butterfly tattoo:
But where? Here on
My arm or my inner
Thigh, small, where
Only the happy few
Might see it? I'll
Never forget that
Moving man, naked to
The waist a prize-
Fight buckle on his
Belt (Panama) and
Flying high on each
Pectoral a bluebird
On tan sky skin. I
Wanted to eat him up:
No such luck. East
28th Street, 1950.
How the roses pass.
I wish I were posing on West 22nd Street, seated
     by a window and the plants,
While your brush makes whorls in your painty
     palette and I watch
The street and kids skim on skateboards: it's
     summer, it's July,
Or else it's winter, December, January, February
     and the kids are gloved and
Bundled up and it's snowball-fighting time: "Gonna
     rub your face in it!" and
Does and one breaks loose and runs crying home.
     In the highest window of
A house across the street a German shepherd rests
     his paws on the sill and
Hangs his head out, gazing down, gazing down,

gazing down and taking in the scene:
These flaming Christmas plants bring to mind
    Joel Poinsett: must read up on
Him: and in September (it isn't winter, it's
    summer, it's July) I'll see your
New crop of work: I'll like that: are you staying
    off the sauce? Remember what
The doctor said: I am: remembering and staying
    off: mostly it's not
So hard (indeed): did you know a side effect of
    Antabuse can be to make
You impotent? Not that I need much help in that
    department these days: funny,
I remember walking under the palms on liberty in
    1943 with a soldier
I had just picked up and in my sailor suit some-
    thing stony as the
Washington Monument I wanted to hide from the
    officer coming toward me: I
Guess I was afraid he'd see it, get the picture
    of what was about to and in fact
Did happen, and send me back to base. Key West!
    the beautiful white houses
With the louvered upstairs, downstairs porches,
    the heavy oaks densely hung
With Spanish moss, the tall blue-blacks with
    hauteur and disdain, beyond
The chain fence, in their eyes and carriage:
    "Stay out of Jungle Town" "You
Bet I will": the barracuda and the angelfish,
    stars like the Koh-i-noor
And a full moon reflecting back the star-encrusted
    sea, a face-
Enveloping moon I want to see again casting
    black velvet shadows of
The palms and broad banana leaves. But that son
    of a bitch, that soldier:

He was trade. I was much too young in those days
    for that jazz and walked
Away and left him to bring himself off any way
    he chose, by fist, I suppose.
Sitting typing in my undershorts on this chilly
    soggy morning while the rain
Comes and goes: I'd like to live in T-shirt
    and undershorts,
Bare feet, my Danish silver chain, a gift from
    the one who mattered most,
Gone as last year's roses (Souvenir de la
    Malmaison): that I'll never again
Fall asleep with my head on his chest or shoulder
    that kind of bugs me and
Pictures linger clearly: outside the Hotel Chelsea
    he stood across
The street, in tweed, a snappy dresser, feet
    apart, head turned
In an Irish profile, holding an English attaché
    case, looking for
A cab to Madison Avenue, late, as usual, looking
    right out of a bandbox,
As usual. I won't make a catalogue of all the
    times we were together I
Remember: just one more: slim and muscular you
    come out of the shower,
Wrap a towel around your waist and lean on the
    washbasin with one
Hand, then squirting Noxzema shaving foam to
    smear on your
Sharp-boned face and shave. Wilkinson Injector.
    Green eyes in the
Medicine-chest mirror. You said, "I'm sorry:
    everything just got too
Fucked up. Thank you for the book." That's
    what I get. Was it worth it?
On the whole, I think it was. Toot-toot-

tootsie, goodbye.
The low and seamless cloud is over us, the
    all there is to it
Morning sky: again: day after day but today
    is breakthrough day, the sun
Burns through then goes away then returns
    more brightly, a breezy coolness
At the window and at my back stirs the
    Peperomia, the grass here and across
The street (HOUSE FOR SALE) almost glares: a
    lawn mower makes its heavy hum
Advancing and retreating in a dance, a reel,
    sweet Jesus, it's my nephew
Mike mowing his granny's lawn. "Mike, come in
    and have a Coke" "I
Will, Uncle Jim, soon as I'm done," he wears an
    Ace bandage on an elbow where
He cracked it canoeing at scout camp last week.
    He likes to
Ski, he likes to wrestle, he has a ten-speed
    bike, he likes to shoot small
Game in the fields and wood behind their house
    on the other side of town
Where you get the best views of the sunsets,
    violet laced with orange and
White fritters: kimono colors: oh, I saw those
    jays again at dawn
Tearing at something white and the something white
    was a white petunia, the jays
Are real workers at their job and the petunia row
    is shredded almost
All away: tall and sentinel above what's left
    of them a dense row of lilies
Long in bud, soon to bloom with their foxy
    adolescent girl smell: repellent
Yet sexy and crotch-calling: Baudelaire, I'd like
    to share a pipe with

You (we could both wear gloves, for fear of
        the itch) and I would be a nineteenth-
Century dandy dude smelling strongly of vanilla
        bean: did you know that
Vanilla is an orchid? And so are you, my cutie,
        reeking of poppers
In the parlor car, Southampton bound: you must have
        had quite a night of it
At the sauna: tell me what you did: you did? Oh wow.
        "Jimmy," you said, "don't tell
Anyone you have syphilis," "Of course I'm going to
        tell X, I have no secrets
From him; anyway, I've already told Y and Z, they
        didn't take it big and
Laughed when I said they should have blood tests."
        I told
X in a skylit room and he was, to my surprise, cross,
        unsympathetic, in fact
Disgusted: it was all out of his range, the range of
Things that happen to folks you know: "You must
        be more careful
About catching syphilis," "When you had your accident
        I didn't say be
More careful of getting hit by trains," and "If
        I'm to have any sex
At all to do so I must run a risk" (back in the
        Turkish-bath days): no
One stayed mad, I got well, and when I went to my
        doctor for my last
Injection I walked in on his wake. Within a week
        his aide had killed
Himself, his wife had burned to death in her living
        room, all on morphine
And my doctor had cared, had tried to care for
        them all, others too.
In the cool insistent sun of this changed day—
        Scotland has gone away, western

New York is, it seems, back to stay—beneath the north
    window I see out of when I
Look left, large leaves of Solomon's-seal make light
    and shadows on themselves
Moved by air, the air is like the gray-haired striding
    slim-waisted
Man who went through the automatic doors yesterday
    afternoon at the store ahead
Of me: I wanted to tap his shoulder and say, "Excuse
    me, I'm sure that we have
Met: were you in the class of '41?" Instead I grabbed
    a cart, went wheeling
up and down the aisles trying to get a front view of
    him and see how he was
Hung and what his face was like. But when I reached
    my goal he was wearing
(I surmise) Jockey shorts (I curse the inventor of
    Jockey shorts) and his face
Was weathered like someone who plays golf a lot,
    not handsome but a kind of
Face I like: he was smelling and squeezing honeydews
    (I'll be your honeydew,
Your Persian melon) when suddenly he raised
    his head and passed
Me, as on a tray, a plain and questioning
    straightforward hostile look: I
Dropped a green bell pepper (10¢) in the cart and
    went wheeling on:
"What am I forgetting?": when I was young I didn't go
    for guys my age, I sought
Out men his age (fifty-five?) about the age I am
    now, but now men my age are not
Interested in me, they seek out beauties, blue-eyed,
    blond and tanned, or in other
Colorations, the cult of youth, I'd like to kick them
    all: there's no democracy:
"Time to retire" when I saw a broad-beamed lady

202

also frown and give me a
Different kind of look: "I know your face . . . aren't
    you . . ." you're
Right, dear, you sat in front of me in senior English
    or was it chemistry
Or French or study hall? I grab a ton of milk and
    head for the express check-
Out lane, first shoving the unwanted bell pepper
    in among some
Dog food. The man had vanished. What a great love
    ours might have been, doing
It on the golf course at 2 a.m. (he was clearly
    married, all the good ones
Are). At the hardware store I bought an onion
    chopper, glass and shrill orange
Plastic, and an old-fashioned mousetrap, up-dated
    with a scented, simulated
Piece of wooden cheese. I hate mousetraps: waking
    in the night to hear
The thrashing crashing struggle on the kitchen
    floor, the hideous trapped
Scream of pain: and I'm the one who will have
    to deal with it: drowning? an
Elephant gun? Besides, what's wrong with mice? A
    few mouse turds
Are soon swept up. Now rats, rats are another story.
    This day, I want to
Send it to you, the sound of stirring air, soft
    sunlight, quivering trees
That shake their needles and leaves like fingers
    improvising on a keyboard
Scriabin in his softest mood, and the wind
    rises and it all goes Delius,
The sky pale and freshly washed, the blue flaked
    off here and there and
Showing white, flat and skimpy clouds haunting
    a bright green, a soft blue day.

I'm sorry the full moon is past, still, there
　　are shadows on the grass
Fit to lie in; study the leaves or blades and let
　　the scurrying
Black ants traverse your arm, your hand: the dog
　　next door got in the trash
Again: a black and husky chummy fellow, him I
　　can't get mad at. The days
Go by, soon I will go back, back to Chelsea, my
　　room that faces south
And the ailanthus tree wound with ivy, my records,
　　stacks and stacks of them,
Spohr's Double Quartet, Ida Cox, and sit in your
　　parlor on the squishy chairs
On West 22nd Street, the Fauré Second Piano quartet,
　　mirrors and pictures
On the walls: next weekend I hear you're going
　　To Sagaponack for a double
Birthday party and half of it is you: 37 meets
　　49: many happy returns to
You and You and years and years to come: today
　　is a year, a morning, this
Morning was a year, I got up at six? six-thirty?
　　on the grass there lay one
Streak of morning light: the days and their different
　　lights: when I
Was a child in Washington they took me to the
　　theater to see Edward
Everett Horton in *Springtime for Henry* (in which
　　that master of the double
Take toured for years: catch him with Helen Broderick
　　and Fred and Ginger
And Eric Blore in *Top Hat*) and when the curtain
　　went up on the second
Act my breath caught: it was the light: I'd seen
　　that light before in Chevy
Chase: an empty living room

with chintz:
An old theatrical effect: then someone entered:
    left, right, center? Who
Cares? It wasn't the play I liked—too young to
    know what it was
All about—it was the magic of the rising
    of the curtain and the slanting
In of dusty golden autumn light. And earlier,
    before the divorce, at Virginia
Gold's family farm in stony Virginia, I went
    paddling bare-ass in a
Brook with another little boy: when I got back
    my mother raised heck:
"I told you *not* to go in that brook" "I didn't
    go in the brook" (how
Did they always know? I thought I was such an
    accomplished liar: I
Became a pretty good one later) "Then why are
    your B.V.D.s on
Inside out?" Unanswerable questions. The big
    barn had been struck by
Lightning and burned down. The men were rebuilding
    it: Mrs Gold fed the
Chickens and let me help: the pigs were big and
    to be kept away from: they
Were mean: on the back porch was the separator,
    milk and cream, luxurious
Ice cream, the best, the very best, and on the
    front porch stood a spinet
Whose ivory keys had turned pale pink: why? There
    was only one
Book on the parlor table and it was Lindbergh's
    We: how can I know that?
I couldn't read: someone told me no doubt and
    no doubt it was Virginia
Gold, she was a schoolteacher, I'm pretty sure.
    I don't remember much about

Her except her blueberry muffins and later
    she and my mother had
A terrible quarrel on the telephone—the
    harsh and hateful voices made me
Sick—and never met again. Mr Gold drove us
    in a Model T or
Touring car to catch a train and in the Union
    Station my father, Mark, was waiting
For us: heavy, jolly, well-read man, you've
    been gone a long time—
More than thirty years—and time I suppose
    has swept all the Golds
Under the carpet too. But I forgot: one of
    the best days at the farm:
The women put their bonnets on and I went
    with them up a hot dusty road
To fields with rock outcrops (watch out for
    snakes) and gathered poke-
Weed. Fried ham and pokeweed, and, in New
    Brunswick, a side order of
Fiddlehead ferns. Europe bores me: it's too
    late: I mean I'm too late:
I've been there: no, it isn't that: I love
    architecture more than anything,
Bernini and Palladio and Laurana, a certain
    church in Venice, Mauro
Coducci, Buonarroti's windows on the Farnese
    Palace. Architecture?
What about Donatello and della Quercia,
    Canova and Verrocchio, the Pisani?
Music and dancing, acting: the Grand Canal in
    autumn after a week of rain:
The water pours from mountains and turns milky-
    green, the tourists
And the vapid rich leave and you are left with
    infinite riches,
The Istrian stone with the silver-pink cast to

206

it of Georg Arends that
After a rainstorm enflames itself: no: that's
        the bricks (Istrian
Stone and bricks contrasted) that become petals
        of roses, blossoming
Stone. Black gondolas glide by, the sure-footed
        gondoliers bending and
Leaning on their poles, wearing green velvet
        slippers. On Diaghilev's
Tomb a French count left his calling
        card: more suitable
Than withering flowers. I left only a glance
        and a thought.
But Europe—split, twisted, shivering-leaved
        olive trees,
Grapevines strung high in swags between
        poplar trees—Europe isn't
Home. The rolling farmland of New York, or better still
        Maine and its coast and
Bays and islands, New Brunswick, Nova Scotia,
        white clapboard
Houses with red geraniums inside sparkling
        windows, eating lobster, greedily,
Vermont with a New Year gift of hellish cold and
        deep, glittering, blinding
Snow: lie face down in it and die: please don't
        die, get up and go inside
Where the logs snap and crackle and smoke and
        give off their
Heart- and flesh-warming smell: the beautiful
        humorous white whippet
No longer lies, legs in the air, on the green
        velvet Victorian couch under
Mrs Appleyard's painting on velvet of an épergne
        full of fruit: can't one,
Just one, mortal person or animal be immortal,
        live

Forever? Not shriveling like Tithonus, not in
    an improbable Cloud-Cuckoo-
Land you'd like to but can't quite believe in:
    ageless, immortal, speedy
Here in Vermont, chasing rabbits, having a wonderful
    roll in the horse shit:
"Yum! Good!" "Whippoorwill! *What* have you done?"
    (His Master's Voice), the
Graceful tail curling down and in between his
    legs: can a tail curl down
Shamefacedly? His could, and he could strew
    a house with trash, leave
An uninviting mess on stairs: "Surprise! Surprise!"
    or the night I came in
And found between me and my bed the contents
    of a three-pound box
Of the choicest candy: a cheval-de-frise of
    chocolates: and,
Most beautiful of all, on a long long lawn running,
    racing as whippets
Are bred to do and leaping straight into
    Kenward's arms, who
Casually closed them: quite an act! (That moment in
Serenade when the dancer soars across the stage,
    turns, legs in extension,
Full in the male dancer's face and he
    clasps her
By the waist. They freeze. Patricia. Nicky.)
    Yes, that whippet is
The one I nominate for terrestrial immortality:
    "They say that when
The moon is dark a thin white dog goes racing up
    and down Apple Hill,
You see the white scuts of deer fly off to hide,
    the skunks
Scuttle under maidenhair, a pond reflects the night
    and—this is the scary part—

Out of the 'transpicuous gloom' a dog
          named Nightingale
Materializes. I wouldn't live there if you
          paid me." Love, love
Is immortal. Whippoorwill, I know that.
How can I know that? God knows, I may be dumb:
          may be! Was the grave
Lined with moss, a handful of wildflowers tossed
          in, did marl rattle
On a pine box? Or were the ashes scattered
          where milkweed floss
Carry their seeds like little men?
          I see a man
          naked and handsome
          in the pond. I
          see a horse
          lumber up a hill.
          I see tomatoes
          set to ripen on
          a sill. I see
          a dog, two dogs:
          Whippoorwill, of
          the mysterious
          determined inner life:
          "Let me in, let
          me out, let me wind
          myself in a
          crazy quilt," and
          pretty, trembling,
          hysterical Rossignol
          leaping out of
          the back seat of
          an open car never
          to be seen again.
          Rest, lie at rest
          among these hills
          and mountains

in autumn flowing
in maple colors:
crimson, yellow,
orange, green
with white:
ripeness, a resurrection,
leaves, leaves, leaves,
when it's time,
cover us all.
Another day, another dolor. A shopping list:
watermelon wedge
blueberries (2 boxes)
                        (In a far recess of summer
                        Monks are playing soccer)
Bread (Arnold sandwich)
Yogurt (plain)
Taster's Choice
Brim
Milk (2 qts)
Whipping cream
Dispoz-A-Lite
Lee Riders
Something for Sunday dinner
Blue Top-Siders (10½)
Little apples
Paper napkins?
Guerlain Impériale
Steak
Noxzema medicated shave foam
Alka-Seltzer
Baume Bengué
K-Y
There is not one store in this good-sized village
      that will deliver. Guess
I'll have to call a cab: while I ate my oatmeal
      and read the *Courier Express*
(that fireman who's been doing it with adolescent

girls got twenty-five years:
"Sodomy in the first degree; sodomy in the second
      degree: sodomy in the third
Degree": what's that all about? and a theater group
      is putting on a show called
Bullets in the Potato Salad) it began heartily
      to rain: not in drops,
In liquid shafts driving into the lawn and earth
      drilling holes, beating up
The impatiens, petunias, lilies (whose cock-like
      buds are turning orange) and
The bluey-purple flowers like larkspur only not
      so nice (there is a bowl
Of everlasting on my dressing table: I'd like to
      dump it out: I hate the feel
Of their papery stiff petals: why feel it then?
      Can't help myself, feel, feel).
Rain! this morning I liked it more than sun, if I were
      younger I would have
Run out naked in it, my hair full of Prell, chilled
      and loving it, cleansed,
Refreshed, at one with quince and apple trees. As it was
      it was enough to
Sit and eat and watch it, wet weavings of a summer morning,
      and try to stop
My mother from slamming every window and shutting out
      the smell,
The sweet, sweet, sweet smell of morning rain, in
      your nose, on bare skin.
"Don't shut that window: it isn't coming in." "Well,
      it *might* come in and
I'm the one who will have to clean it up." Slam. I
      open it again: "This
Rain will last about thirty seconds (it did), I'm watching
      it and if
It starts to blow in I'll close the window." "See
      you do: and you can

Mop it." I read about Brian Goodell the great
    Olympic teen-
Age swimmer and feel like smashing dishes (never
    forget the morning when
Mother yelled, "Don't you *dare* throw that light bulb
    at me!" I didn't: I
Smashed it on the wall: when you're sound asleep
    and someone yanks the
Covers off . . .). Two people obstinate as mules, who
    love each other: I wonder
Though, do I really love anybody? I think I'll can
    it with this love
Stuff for a while; when a friend made a joke
    about death I
Laughed too and said, "I'm ready to go any
    time." "Why, Jimmy!" she said:
"No, I mean it." I wish it was 1938 or '39 again
    and Bernie was sleeping
With me in the tent at the back of the yard
    the time we got up
In the starry night and went downhill,
    down Olean Road, downhill again
And through the pasture where the cows coughed
    and exhaled warm breath,
Barefoot among the cow flops (Dutchman's
    razors) and stands of thistles and
Buttercups the cows won't eat (if you're not
    a farm boy, coming up against
A cow the size of a battleship is not unnerving) (now what
    was the name of that boy, the cowfucker,
Who lived down Olean Road? To each his own), sharp cropped
    dewy grass between toes to where Cazenovia
Creek made a big bend and the warm and muddy water was deep
    enough to swim in. Starlighted silent
Ripples as you stroke: the thick black shapes against the
    black are old big trees: Bernie climbs
Up into one and dives: night air is loudly shattered by a
    splash: the crash when the curtain rises

In *La Traviata* on Act One: Violetta is "having an at home":
    we don't have towels and stand on the clay
Bank to let the air dry us off, grabbing at each other's cock:
    only, it's not that kind of friendship:
Mostly because Bernie was Catholic and worried about confession
    and such: me, in those days I was randy most
All the time. The back doorbell rings: it's the laundry
    lad, he's got my slacks, "a buck twenty-five,"
He's funny-faced, skinny and muscular, red-gold hair, and, sigh,
    wears a broad plain wedding ring. I make
Myself sound like a dirty old man, a hound, always on the sniff:
    the truth is I haven't had sex in over a year
And a half: as Ethel sang: *When the only man in the world*
                You care about
                Talks of somebody else
                And
                Walks
                Out . . . (Mr Cole Porter, and I
                      May be misquoting)
Bob, who am I kidding? In some ways you were bright and gifted,
    in others, you were one dumb ox. I insist,
Though, you were gifted, much more than, somehow, you could
    let yourself know: spending it in trivial
Ways: no: hiding it under the sod, where you couldn't find
    or use it. Love letters are said to make dull
Reading: I have one from you that's as good as Byron, and on
    it you wrote in your weird hand, "I'm not
Going to read this over because if I do I'll tear it up." I
    keep that letter, but only once have I taken it
Out and read it: ouch: cologne in a shaving cut. Where
    are you? I don't want to know (yes I do)
How are you? (who cares?) did you and your wife divorce (that,
    I am curious about: splitting after twenty-three
Years?) who got the pretty farmhouse in Jersey where the yellow
    Japanese iris I gave you flourish? and why did
You keep saying no to a clump of big white chrysanthemums?
    Splendid against deep grass at the end of August, almost
Unkillable, a perfect perennial for a lazy gardener, which you

were (so am I), again, old chum, goodbye: I
Did a better job with Donald, I winkled him out of an antique
    shop and back into life and I didn't know I'd
Done it until he told me: they break your heart and then they
    thank you: your heart! They break your
Balls and say, "You really helped me: you know, *I*
    was in *love* with you; I think": the first,
The very first, Paul, the one in high school,
    later said, after that winter of
Silent midnight walks in the deep snow, "I couldn't take it:
    it was too heavy: you put on too much
Pressure: but I kept that letter you wrote me in that empty
    freezing house: it touched me." Every time
He thought he'd got out from under I thought of a new trick:
    a dozen dark red roses for his mother (she,
She was nice), "Paul, I'm very fond of Jimmy: I've invited him
    to dinner to help celebrate my birthday," that
Must have pissed him off: I went though and enjoyed myself:
    with Paul's parents, surprisingly, I was
Never shy, bragging about my Schuyler descent and who Alexander
    Hamilton married (it wasn't me): or the dark
Summer night when Bernie—we were getting old, planning to
    go to Guatemala, we still slept in the tent—and
I crept into their darkened house and up the stairs and into Paul's
    room and woke him up: he was furious but got
Dressed and came out to the Roycroft Inn and got mildly drunk
    on gin and Squirt: I knew it would work:
Paul was nuts about Bernie. All Bernie ever said about him was, "I
    saw your heartthrob the other night
At Kleinhans Music Hall: I knew him by his piggy little eyes."
    Then one day (snap your fingers, tap your toes)
It was over: I passed him on the street and looked at him un-
    sheepishly and said, "Hi, Paul," he was startled into saying
"Hello" for the first time in a year: later, not much later but later,
    comparing notes on our first acquaintance
With queer ("gay," if you prefer) New York, he said, "One night
    I hocked my one good suit so I could go to the

214

One Two Three Club and hear Roger Stearns play Cole Porter: it's
   cheap if you sit at the bar": "I'm well
Aware: did you get picked up?" "I'm not telling": which meant
   he didn't: he was not good-looking enough to
Make it in that kept-boy crowd (between sets Roger Stearns sat at
   his own table with the most beautiful sailor
I ever saw—on the nights when I went there). We were sitting on
   a sofa, side by side, and Paul reached out and
Put his hand on my crotch and fiddled with my fly (the crust) and
   got the horselaugh of his life. He sure did
Have little piggy eyes. "Let's take a walk to Stinking Pond."
   "O.K.," he said: he was a realist in a
Sickening sort of way. Years afterward he called me at the Museum
   and said, "Let's get together": "I'd love to
But I'm going out of town: a Museum show I'm working on." Finis:
   Paul, with the peculiar cock, short, thick,
Twisted, lumpy, like a piece of rotted rope (give it to the
   oakum pickers), I'll remember you one way,
Sitting in front of me in I wonder which class, with beautiful
   Patricia sitting in front of you and leaning
Back while you slowly combed her hair. You were also Luther
   Smeltzer's pet: that I did not like: it made
Me jealous: Mr Smeltzer, who opened windows for me on
   flowering fields and bays where the water greenly danced,
Knifed into waves by wind: the day he disclosed William Carlos
   Williams to us, writing a short and seemingly
Senseless poem on the blackboard—I've searched the collected
   poems and am never sure which it is (Wallace
Stevens, Marianne Moore, Elizabeth Bishop, I found for myself:
   even then, there's a chance that I was somewhat
Smarter than Luther Smeltzer: "Who, where, when, what and
   why": his journalism lessons were not too novel)—
And telling us about a book that based its narrative on Homer,
   "stream of consciousness," Dorothy Richardson,
After class I asked where could I get that book? "Chuckle chuckle:
   when you're in college it will be time enough."
In my quiet way I never have cared much for horse shit so I

215

went into Buffalo to Otto Ulbrich's book
Shop, where John Myers, to whom the arts stand indebted, then
    worked as a clerk: "You look interesting:
Here's a copy of my new little magazine, *Upstate*." I bought
    my book and hitchhiked home. Hiding what
It was like from old book burner, my stepfather, was an easy
    trick: "I have to write a book report: it's
A story about poor people in Ireland. Dublin." "Probably
    stinks to high hell it's so filthy. Here,
Let me see that book": he leafed through it, not knowing where
    to look for Molly Bloom, and tossed it at me:
"Still can't catch: go mow the lawn": I mowed the lawn. One
    day in American history class—taught by Miss
Pratt, so old in 1940 she still wore her hair in a pompadour,
    combed up over a rat—I was deep in the clotted
Irish rhetoric (as Frank O'Hara said about Dylan Thomas, "I can't
    stand all that Welsh spit") when a member of the
Football team leaned over: "That's the book that tells it like
    it is: it is hot—how did *you* get hold of it?"
"I guess the same way you did": bright and sassy: but to be
    spoken to by a football player and on equal
Terms! and the shock that anyone would think I was reading it
    as porn! This was art, this was truth, this
Was beauty: it was also laborious and dull, but I plowed on.
    When I first knew John Ashbery he slipped me
One of his trick test questions (we were looking at a window
    full of knitted ribbon dresses): "I don't think
James Joyce is any good: do you?" Think, what did I think! I
    didn't know you were *allowed* not to like James
Joyce. The book I suppose is a masterpiece: freedom of choice
    is better. Thank you, "Little J.A. in a
Prospect of Flowers." Last evening Mike mowed the lawn again:
    in the silken dawn each leaf and blade and
Needle bore its crystal drop, diamonds cut into pearl-shaped
    perfect globes (I never have seen a round
Diamond: why not? I'd like a few to rattle in my pocket: a
    change from rattling change), and the silk
Grew worn, and strained and frayed away and sister sun sipped

the droplets up, not all at once, nor one at
A time, a steady vanishing into the air, sweetening, freshening,
    endewing the day. The days go by like leaves
That fall in fall, not yet, soon, so soon, I feel my death in
    currents of damp air on the back of my neck,
Filtered through a window screen (a casement window screen I
    open in the watches of the night, too lazy
To make it to the john, and take a moonlit piss into the taxus),
    death, my death, over fifty years and that is
What I am building toward. No cremation, thanks, worm food,
    soil enrichment, mulch. Another morning and
I hand you a hammered silver brooch dripping wet, fished from a
    stream. Like a curse in a Greek myth, water,
Not rain in drops or streams, in sheets, water solid as that in
    a swimming pool, massively falls, bending the
Thick-stemmed orange lilies to the ground, turning overmown
    grass back from scorched tan to succulent green,
Curling (I've never noticed this before) maple leaves in on
    themselves like cupped hands and disclosing
Coral petioles: that one red leaf burns on in rain. Here is
    a story about Fairfield Porter. A long long
Time ago he went to paint in "the fairy woods" beyond the
    Double Beaches on Great Spruce Head Island.
He had his portable easel and was wearing, oh, sneakers, shorts,
    a shirt, and a straw hat, a farmer's hat. He
Set up shop and got to work: a view of Bear Island (owned by
    Buckminster Fuller and his sister Rosie). It
Was a fine hot day so Fairfield took off his clothes to enjoy
    what salty breeze there was and went on smearing
Maroger medium on his canvas. From Bear Island put out a
    rowboat or a canoe (I can't remember everything), in
It a couple, a man and a woman, rowing or paddling over the
    sunny bouncing water to the rocky point beyond where
He was painting. Fairfield thought of dressing, but on second
    thought reflected, "This *is* my island." Now he
Was working the pigments into the medium. The couple beached
    in a coign of the rocks, took ashore their lunch
Hamper, and took off their clothes. They were under forty and

217

handsomely built. They ate their lunch, basked
In the sun and Fairfield forgot them as he went on painting.
  After a rest, the stranger got up and left
His mate to wander into "the fairy woods" (so named by Fairfield's
  German governess when he was a child: because
Of the silvery beards of moss that hung from the spruce), picking
  and eating wild raspberries that flourish there.
He looked up and the naked men confronted each other. Nobody
  said "Hello," "Goodbye," "Fine day" or "What's
Your name?" He went back to his woman, they dressed and
  returned to Bear Island over the broken gleaming water
Where seals snort and play. Our painter, in his farmer's hat,
  naked as a snake—to quote William Faulkner—
Finished his painting, dressed and ankled home. A winter or two
  later, in brash New York at a party, Fairfield
Noticed a man across the room who kept frowning at him. The
  frown broke into a smile, the smile broke into a grin.
The man pointed at him: "I know you: *you're the man in the hat!*"
  I wish I could say they went on to become the
Best of friends: they didn't, though I suppose they chatted:
  "How's Buckie? How's Rosie?" The painting?
The painting did not turn out one of the best. I think Kenneth
  Koch has it now. Fairfield's life was full of
Incidents like that, and he always carried them off with aplomb.
  Like the time he was canoeing naked and guess
What got sunburned. I like to think of sunburn on a day like
  today, rain in sheets and thunderclaps and
Lightning bolts: in the house the lights flicker on and off:
  we may go up in a sheet of flame: would the
Rain put it out? Who knows? I wish I were paddling an Old Town
  canoe with red and peeling shoulders, bouncing
Over and cutting through curling and icy water: fluent below
  me the giant seaweed called devil's-apron,
While there in the pebbly shallows off Landing Beach John
  gathers mussels to scour and beard with a wire
Brush and an oyster knife, to steam and serve hot in soup plates,
  rich with the salts of the sea. "Do you often

Experience déjà vu, Jimmy?" Edwin asked me. "Why yes," I said
    (old Truthful Thomas). He and George exchanged
A look like a nod, "That proves it," it seemed to say. A lot of
    people believe that a proneness to déjà vu, that
Strange and not unwonderful feeling, I have experienced this, this
    light, these trees, these birds, heard the very
Words you are saying, before, or, it all clicks into place and
    I know what you are about to say: "Please
Stop picking your nose": there, you said it: they see this as
    a symptom of schizophrenia. Hence
The look between wise old Edwin (the color of silvery parchment)
    and knowing George (whose looks were beginning
To go: it wasn't déjà vu that told me they both were hung like
    stallions: only a slight case of experience
I was feeling upset enough God knows, the sanatorium door stood
    agape: but I subscribe to a simpler explanation:
One lobe of the brain registers the event, what in simple reality
    is said or happens or is seen, while the other
Lobe takes it in a split second, an infinitesimal split second
    later, so, in a sense, there is a real déjà vu,
Half the brain has experienced the experience: "I have been here
    before": you have: so know-it-all George and
Edwin can go screw themselves with stalks of glass wheat. Like
    my dream this morning, casting a pall over
This part of the day (why did it have to stop raining?): Donald
    and Roy exchanged a sharp glance, it meant,
"Jimmy is going over the hill": I left in pique and took the
    funicular down the sandstone cliffs: on either
Side businessmen in hats and carrying briefcases were sucking
    each other off in cave-like cubicles: on
The sunless beach, the day after a storm with screaming and
    wheeling gulls and flotsam and jetsam, boards
Stuck with bent and rusty nails and wound with bladder wrack,
    they—the border patrol, the cops, the fuzz—
Stopped me and asked to see my passport: in my mind I could
    see it in a desk drawer in an orange room:
In this land you can't forget your passport: I turned and left
    them and they let me go: I climbed the gritty

Steps which soon penetrated the cliff, the rear entrance to a
    horrible apartment house in the Bronx: to
Go forward could only get worse: I turned and ran back down
    to where the tunnel issued from the cliff:
Below me boys were gathering rocks on the beach with which to
    stone me. I woke up, glad to get out of my
Fresh white bed (usually, I would rather sleep than do anything):
    why should a dream like that fill me with gloom,
A kind of moral hangover: "I may want to die, but at least I
    am still alive?" Was it only yesterday I
Awoke to streaming rain from a dream, a vision, like a late painting
    of Fairfield's, one of the ones of a misshapen
Sun burning through mist over a sliding morning sea? There is
    only one sky: a pewter plate, easily bent:
There are two windows: out one grass may be damp but looks dry;
    out the one to the east, enclosed by trees, the
Broad and pointed leaves of Solomon's-seal are thickly set with
    water drops, as easy to gather as colorless wild
Berries in a cleft in a cliff, as beads on a Patou dance frock:
    green barely freaked with blue and glitter:
Japanese lanterns and serpentine, a confetti blizzard, New Year's
    Eve on a ship at sea, Isham Jones, the Coon Sanders
Band: "And now for your pleasure, ladies and gentlemen, Miss
    Irene Bordoni." Or was it Fifi D'Orsay? Last night,
Driving to the Old Orchard Inn, a flash flood. "Why would a
    bank," my brother asked, "be crazy enough to finance a
House on the flat by a creek where the cellar is bound to flood
    whenever it rains?" Why, indeed? Crossing
Cazenovia Creek the smoothly racing water was almost up to the
    bridge, silent, smooth and creased, a tossed-
Out length of coffee-colored satin. Sadistically, I hoped to
    see a drowned Holstein floating by, a ship of
Furry flesh, its udder like a motor. Drowned Holstein eyes; but
    not a Jersey.

> A better morning comes to pass
> Sunlight buttered on the grass
> Late, late, I lie awake
> Finding pleasure for its own sake

Reading books to pass the time
Print on paper, algae, slime
Until before the dawn a gray
Light breaks, will the day be gay
Or will thunder-stones roll this way?
The former, yes, it may turn out,
Though, no, the latter still come about.
In jinglejangle the day may pass
Light freshly buttered on the grass.
My mother goes off to the podiatrist: she has an ingrown toe-
    nail, it's turning black and looks infected.
My sister-in-law will drive. It hurt so much yesterday
    morning (Sunday) she almost didn't go to church:
Unheard-of. Every weekend we have the same talk:
    "Jim, wouldn't you like to come to church?"
Sometimes I'm rude and say, "Lay off!" Mostly I manage a polite
    "No thank you." "I wish you would." "If
Wishes were horses then beggars could ride. In other words, I'm
    not going to church." "I wouldn't object if you
Want to go to the Catholic church." "If I wanted to go to the
    Catholic church, then I would go. As it happens
I don't." Then why do I carry a rosary with me? Partly because
    a half-mad old woman gave me one (I have two,
As it happens). "You look like a good boy," she said, "here, take
    this": a handful of beads and a dangling crucifix.
I remember the beads slipping through my fingers, decade after
    decade, as the car spun east through Newport, the luxury
Cottages, the cliffs, the sea: what happened to what I thought
    were my resolutions, praying in the Lady Chapel
At St. Patrick's, going to Mass with kindly Father Lynch,
    attending a lecture by Karl Stern, the
Catholic psychiatrist? That was a turn-off: his idea of sin
    was certainly not mine: I have never been
Sure about sin: wrong, yes, but sin and evil, it all gets too
    glib, too easy. Then meeting the head of Fordham,
Like a handsome snake with George Raft hair (only silvery) who
    gave me the fish eye: except for Father Lynch, I can
Live without Jesuits. I can live, it seems, without religion,

though I have never wanted to. Brush in hand,
You've slipped out of my poem: I have such confidence in your
   future, in what you'll create, with paint and
Canvas, Conté crayon and heavy paper, views, faces, a pier glass
   in a long room, a fence hung with roses out a
Garden window: is the stereo playing, and if so, what? *The Ring*,
   Scriabin, moth-wing strokes of Sviatoslav Richter's
Steady fingers? Here, I have no phonograph: television. My mother
   watches (i.e., dozes off) while I sit and read.
The Olympics were fun, marvelous slow-motion underwater shots,
   replays, of swimmers' arms and shoulders
Flexing and pulling and the turn and push off the wall, the
   high divers leaping and spinning to straighten
And smoothly slice the water; the gymnasts, the
   fourteen-year-old girl from Rumania who could do
Anything, anything she pleased, delightful, enchanting, and how
   the crowd went wild when the Russian weight
Lifter broke the Olympic record and then came back to break all
   other existing records: "He's the strongest
Man in the world!" the announcer squealed. "Ladies and
   gentlemen, you've just seen him: the world's strongest
Man!" His voice broke in his excitement. Then horses and hurdles
   and Princess Anne: her horse was too feisty to
Handle: the royal family decorated a box: the Queen, Prince
   Philip, the Prince of Wales, his brothers: a
Close-up shot: my mother came to long enough to ask, "Does the
   Queen have any children?" And dozed off again.
I switch to *Mod Squad*: Adam Greer (played by Tige Andrews) is
   shot by almost invisible poison pellets:
He passes out on the grass: will Peggy Lipton and Clarence
   Williams III find out what the poison is in
Time to obtain an antidote? It seems likely. But what *are* you
   painting, oh you who paint on West 22nd Street?
You're not much of one for writing letters, are you? But then,
   you said you weren't so I can't complain. No
More am I. A bundle of postcards, all of them dull, sits and has
   sat on this desk for days. This afternoon I must

Mail them to you. But it looks like rain! Not again! I wish
    I could send you a bundle of orange lilies
To paint. They stand—and lean—in a row, at the top of a wall
    by the drive. Their anthers are so delicately
Hung that just walking past makes them swing, and if they brush
    your clothes they leave brown stains. Wake up
In the night, after midnight, and open the casement screen and
    study the road gliding downhill, brightly
Lighted by a misshapen half moon, almost white, scooped out of
    lemon ice. How can macadam (or is it called
Asphalt or blacktop?) return this lunar light as a river or
    creek might? On this quiet small-town street,
Whose car coasts quietly up the hill at this late hour? Returning
    from a social event? A night worker going home
To bed? Haven't I seen this car at this hour before? About
    now Mr Talbot used to drive home from the
Buffalo paper for which he wrote a nature column, hunting and
    fishing, the ways of wildlife and what was and
Wasn't burgeoning in fields and swamps. And a little later Joe
    Palmer's sedan slid by, also home from a Buffalo
Paper, a different paper, a rewrite man. Other people live in
    their houses: I know a lot of dead people: I
Don't think of them much. Standing at the window, staring at the
    street, staring at the tree behind which swiftly
Slips the bright twist of a demi-moon, I wish for someone to take
    a nocturnal stroll with, like the moonless
Night on Great South Beach when the waves broke and sprayed us
    and you put your arm around my shoulders and
I thought, "Why can't we walk on like this forever?" Sandy
    sneakers. A car (called the Green Bomb), a drive, home, a
Shower, mussed sheets, bed, sleep as total black at four windows
    melted into the false dawn. Sleep into sunshine,
A Cranshaw melon, and you drive away. I'm chilled at this window
    here in western New York, studying and losing
What's left of the moon: tomorrow night there'll be a bigger
    serving. An August morning, cool and cloudless,
Maple leaves lightly moving, conifers perfectly still, robins

skimming the grass where a fat black dog named
Cornelia just took a dump, a sky not blue but white, up the valley
    from Olean a freight train passes (the distant
Sound of breakers), down the valley toward Olean the loudness and
    smell of diesel trucks, children's voices: shrill:
Back-yard swimming-pool voices. One train rolling toward Buffalo
    right after the other: that's rare: it's
Raining not knowing why. You put down your brush and sit down
    and stare at what you've painted. You light a mild
Cigarette, or a thin cigar. Whoever knows what a painter is
    thinking? Is it obscure and muggy in Chelsea, or light and
Shivery the way it is here? What shall I do with the rest of
    the morning? Shower, shave, write to Barbara,
Go uptown and buy cool milk in waxy cartons? Call my nephew
    and go for a walk? Try to remember what I
Forgot? What I can't remember is the name of my New York
    doctor: "Murray." But Murray what? I must have it
Written down someplace, and if I haven't "you" can tell me.
    When you read this poem you will have to decide
Which of the "yous" are "you." I think you will have no trouble,
    as you rise from your chair and take up your
Brush again and scrub in some green, that particular green,
    whose name I can't remember. Thank God the
Sky cleared: I think it's tonight that the moon is full! Round
    and white as opaque ice, hung from a sky hook
Over a city avenue, tonight, riding slowly up a rural sky, a wheel
    of Gourmandise with the foil peeled off, smelling
Sweetly of cherries, the colorless side of a Royal Anne cherry,
    shedding light perhaps, perhaps with a ring on
The blue-serge night: does a ring around the moon portend rain?
    I bet it does, I bet it will, this dank and
Somber summer. The screen through which I peer cubes all into
    sampler stitches: the suppertime shadows laid
Out in topiary work, a dolphin, a spire, a dog, your name, flat
    and roughly clipped, dark on light, dark green
On bright moon green, the world smells of mown grass. I think
    I see a mountain it must be a cloud: there is

No mountain. Let there be a mountain: Why not? Didn't Long
    Island have a hurricane last night? Didn't
I long to be there in the four-poster bed and hear the shutters
    rattle and the windowpanes whistle and sing
And the thunder of the surf, wind in the giant plane tree? And
    to get up in a cleared-off day and go to the beach
And the dunes and see the scattered wrack, fish and weed and
    (always) some cast-up surprise: fishing
Gear, net, an ominous object of red and orange plastic, breakers
    rough, dull and full of sand and the sinus-
Clearing oceanic smell. Dunes carved into new shapes, salt
    air, combing through the cut grass, beach plum,
Unkillable rosa rugosa. Maybe a big beach cottage has had its
    foundation of sand eroded by water and wind:
Toppling, ready to tumble: why so much pleasure in wrack and
    ruin? A house falls into the sea: my heart
Gives a jump. But the paper says the eye of the hurricane and
    the moon-drawn high of the tide did not coincide:
Probably nothing much happened. What a gyp. Or better this way?
    At least I needn't feel guilty for my pleasure
In wrack and ruin. Suppertime shadows sneaking over the lawn,
    a buzz saw slicing a tree into portions, cars
Coming up the hill to dinner (they all eat Jell-O), me smoking
    and you painting: no: cleaning your brushes
(Though about that you are not quite so scrupulous as some I
    know): what's for dinner? Shrimp croquettes?
Barbara Guest sent me a card, "Architectural Perspective, Italian,
    late 15th Century," that gave me a pang, that makes
Me long to take you to that loveliest land and we could visit
    Vicenza, walk up the drive to the Villa
Rotunda, the building with the noblest profile in the world,
    see the cut of the flights of steps as you
Slowly perambulate through grass scattered with pecking white
    chickens, go to the hilltop wall and look
Down at the fields below, where peacocks fan their tails. I doubt
    it will happen: still, there's our projected trip
To Washington and the National Gallery, that's to look forward to.

Paintings are such a pleasure: can I tempt you
With Cleveland and Boston and Baltimore? California, frankly,
   is just too far. Suppertime shadows, my gastric
Juices are beginning to flow. Barbara writes, "I can see you working
   & poking your head outdoors in the evening—or
Taking a late walk—" she may be right. She was right, I poked
   my head out of doors after supper (beef in
Tomato sauce—ick) and there the tiger lilies were, in a row
   above a low wall above the drive in which grew
A few more tiger lilies, reddish orange, petals turning back,
   dark brown pollen, no scent, the strong
Thick stems beaded with round black seeds. Further on, past
   the birdbath, its basin partly filled with
Gunk (childhood memory: "Put down that book and go scrub the
   birdbath"), to the apple and quince trees
Looking so old, so unkempt: I remember planting them, they were
   just seedlings, or do I mean saplings? Now
They stand, unpruned, unbearing, smothered in swags of Concord
   grape leaves lightly, heavily moving like the
Heave of the sea, leaf over leaf, and hung among them cloudy
   green bunches of grapes. I would like to wait
And see them empurple, I would like to wait and taste that
   particular taste, so sweet when they're really ripe: did
They tell you that if you swallow them the seeds will catch in
   your appendix and give you peritonitis? I
Always swallow them, don't you? Letting the oozy grape meat slide
   down my throat like an oyster: grapes, oysters
And champagne: bliss is such a simple thing. A faded photograph
   shows (it says in pencil on the back), "This is
What the woods are like": white-stemmed trees, smudges (needles),
   rough soft grass. (I made limeade: sticky
Fingers: I drink and type: sticky keys.) Those woods, that
   island and the bay, I won't forget them soon,
Nor that same moon I saw last night hang in glory over this small
   hill I used to see ride, embosomed, in the fullness
Of the sky it lit etching the tall, still spruce and casting its
   light on the rippled water that led off and off

To ocean and to where you cannot see: to go out through the
    dining porch among the daisies and the crags
And moon-bathe. Have you ever swum at night in water so cold it's
    like plunging into a case of knives, your quickly
Moving limbs dripping with moonstones, liquid moonstones? I
    turned my back and this small green world went shadowless:
The nimbus is back at four in the afternoon: no moon tonight.
    Before dawn I woke and made my oatmeal, orange juice and
Coffee and thought how this poem seems mostly about what I've
    lost: the one who mattered most, my best friend, Paul
(Who mattered least), the Island, the California wildflower paper,
    the this, the that, Whippoorwill, buried friends,
And the things I only write between the lines. What can one write
    between the lines? Not one damn thing. Look over
Your shoulder, into the future: one thing I want to see is heavy
    snow falling in Chelsea, to walk in it, snow
Blowing in my face, from where I live to where you live, to stomp
    the snow off in your vestibule, to punch your bell,
To hear the buzzer buzz, to push the door and see the open inside
    door and you smiling there: "Hi-ee: how *are*
You? What will it be? The usual?" A tall cold glass of Vichy.
    Winter in New York, when the big wet flakes
Stream horizontal. (Funny, I haven't beat my meat in days—why's
    that?) I think it may rain again tonight—a
Shower, a smattering—suddenly I feel it in the breeze that
    lifts the paper on which I type. I smell
It, faintly, the fresh faint smell of coming summer rain. I
    used to climb out my first-floor bedroom
Window, naked, into it: the slippery wet bathmat grass, the
    rain, both cool and warm, plastering down
My hair, rain running all over me as I danced or stood in it,
    the long persistent tongues of summer rain:
"Want a trip around the world?" "OK" And so it did, the
    licking, bathing summer rain. Another dawn as
Gray as hands that shovel pea coal into an Aga cookstove: under
    it, the walks and road shine slick as though
Greased with Vaseline: in the middle of the night, deep in

the dark of that time of the morning when it
Seems light will never return and only a weight of black go on
    and on, what a storm we had, the lancing of the
Rain, the thunder cracks and lightning bolts happening as one: I
    thought the house was struck, or at least a
Nearby tree, my bedroom lighting up in flares like the strobe
    light in a discotheque. You bet I didn't go out
In that for any sexy rain bath: no-siree-bob. The air is cool
    but heavy, clammy, robins are garnering earth-
Worms from the lawn: I see one long worm wriggle as it's
    swallowed. Early, so early, it lightly rains again: or is
It drops showering down from leaves on other leaves? So early
    that the morning paper hasn't come yet: Eric
Larsen brings it, he's about thirteen, with yellow Scandinavian
    hair: first his older brother passes, with
Papers for houses further up the hill, then, at, oh, seven or
    so, Eric trudges across the grass to leave the
Courier Express on the brick steps: "Good morning, Eric," "Good
    morning," gruff, but with a shy smile, and I
Sit down to coffee and the news: the Republican Convention, rapes
    and muggings, arson: arson—I don't know why—
Is very big on the Niagara Frontier. A barn burner has been busy
    on these summer nights: the Courier keeps
Pointing out he doesn't seem to want to hurt anybody, he just
    wants to see the wood flame and roar up into
The night sky (although one herd of Holsteins were roasted in
    their stalls: perhaps our friend didn't know
That they were there?): I'm glad his meat is not small white
    clapboard houses. A day comes in a month, in a season, and
You wish it were some other month, another season. I never have
    liked August much, I wish it were September,
October, I wish it were the fall. Falling leaves, glittering
    blue skies, in the country, late goldenrod
And asters, in the city, a crackle to the air, a crackle, and
    at the same time a balminess. The Bluebird
Laundry truck comes and goes (I missed my chat with the freckled
    driver), there are small dandelions scattered

228

On the lawn: no, yellowed Euonymus leaves blown down by last
    night's storm. With all that sudden force, not
A single lily stalk was bent or broken. They stand in rows in
    metal strength and curve their petals back
And give a point to August. "All he cares about are leaves and
    flowers and weather": and who are you, which
Maple are you I mean, the one who curves its leaves like hands
    disclosing pink palms, growing in clusters on
Branches with silver bark and already bearing five, six, colored
    (a light rich red) leaves? A silver bark?
A swamp maple: isn't that the one whose leaves turn first? I
    think it is, I remember one, deeply blazing
Full in late summer, growing in swampy ground where the waterfall
    tumbled and tinkled down to feed the beaver pond.
The other evening my mother and I were watching TV in the living
    room when something fell, a metal clang on the
Back stoop. I went and put the outside lights on and looked:
    the trash-can lid had been knocked off and
Perched on the can full of trash was the biggest raccoon I've
    ever seen: he turned his head and looked me
In the eye, hopped down and walked sedately off into the shrubs.
    I put the lid back on and dragged the can into
The vestibule. "I wish you had seen him," I told my mother, "he
    was beautiful: he was so *big!*" "Maybe he
Was a dog," she said, deep in her program. I don't know why,
    but that breaks me up, like telling someone
You've seen a rat, and they say, "Maybe it was a fat mouse."
    I'd love to have picked him up and held him,
Only, frankly, I thought he might incline to bite. I would like
    to put food out for him, but how could I know
He was eating it and not the dogs that swarm around this hill?
    The dogs, they get enough to eat at home.
The mail comes, the mailman smiles and goes away in blue, slowly
    and steadily, to the next house behind a screen
Of trees and shrubs (spruce, forsythia). Letters from Kenward,
    Trevor, Anne Porter, Darragh and "Domaine de St.
Esteve, Lambesc," in other words, Anne Dunn, who writes:

It was nice having the Hazans here but unfortunately I had to leave midway through their visit as my brother was dying and I wanted to be with him. In so far as dying of cancer is bearable his death was, his wife, two daughters and myself never left him, until the last 24 hours the grandchildren and the dogs ran in and out as usual, he was heavily doped but conscious and felt reassured by our being there. I must admit his dying was pretty harrowing, I have never sat holding someone's hand before as they "take off." After the funeral Rodrigo and I went to Lincoln to see the cathedral which was one of Philip's last wishes so we filled in for him, on the way there we went to the Peak District which was beautiful, rolling country flecked with stone walls and dreamy cows, we stayed at Bakewell and ate Bakewell tarts, also visited Chatsworth Gardens which are sensational and put the Himalayas to shame, the scale is so cunningly manipulated, extraordinary growths of giant cow parsley by rushing streams, I wish you had been there. The temperature was in the 90's which you wouldn't have liked much. I fell in love with the Lincolnshire wolds. We came back by the Boston Stump (St. Botolph's) restored by the good people of Boston, Mass, and Ely whose cathedral I really loved, much more so than Lincoln.
How English, the children and the dogs—especially the dogs—
    running in and out of the room where the man—
The son, brother, husband, father, grandfather—lay slowly dying.
    "In the midst of life we are in death, in the
Midst of death we are in life": I know how harrowing it must
    have been for you, but, though I'm not much of
A mystic, I'm sure in that long last handclasp he gave you
    something: not just love, the electric flow of his failing
Power: a gentle charge: and in exchange took with him from your
    physical grip all that you felt for him all those
Years, condensed in a red pulsation. And what a fine memorial, to
    take a pleasant pilgrimage he would have liked to
Take: Lincoln, the Lincolnshire wolds, the Peak District, Ely, the
    gardens at Chatsworth (Paxton, surely?): yes,
I wish I had been with you. Perhaps one day I will. Dear, dear
    Anne. What is "the Isle of Ely"? Is there

Really an island? And when next you come to 185 East 85th, please
      bake me a Bakewell tart: I'm sure there's a
Recipe in that Florence White cookbook I gave you (and I would
      not mind a Grassy Corner pudding). Here,
Stillness, and a car honks twice, lunchtime stillness: all
      morning we lived in a barbershop, the
Perpetual power mowers shaving away the relentlessly growing
      grass. Peace and quiet, a sullen, sultry sun
Slants under a leaden sky. A fat woman in a loose dress pads
      down the hill: who's she? A big white
Butterfly zigzags by, and a smaller yellow one: distantly,
      a dog barks, nearby, a young child yammers
And squawks (the neighbors have children and grandchildren
      visiting), I subside into the quiet of my
Room, annunciated by the rapid ticking of my cheap alarm clock.
      (The phone bill came: last month I spent
A hundred dollars on long-distance calls: I must be bored here,
      without my friends: I shouldn't do it, but
Calling France is so much fun: "Give me the overseas operator":
      oh to be rich, to do all you want, to visit
Chatsworth and Bathurst, in New Brunswick: oh, you know.)
      August half over, and another dawn that is no dawn, a
Mezzotint of a morning: how I used to pore over Pennell's *Etchers
      and Etching*, plate after plate, weird, smeared,
Sooty, scratched: Rembrandt, Whistler, Goya, Félicien Rops, an
      Irishman whose name I forget, a stream densely
Banked by unmown grass: water, sunlight, succulence, a curve.
      I'd like to collect etchings of the post-Whistler
Period, minor works by minor masters, evocative and fresh. My
      heavy naked calves are etched with hairs, worn
Off on the inner side where my legs rub against my jeans. On
      this miserable Sunday morning ("Jim, are you
Sure you wouldn't like to come to church?") I like to sit in this
      Hitchcock chair and idly pull my foreskin—I'm
Sitting in my undershorts—and drink iced tea and smoke and have
      a passing sexy thought for someone I won't ever
Have—the eyes, the wide slope of the shoulders, the thighs—and

231

let tunes play in my head: Carly Simon singing
"Anticipation," Mado Robin singing "Fascination," golden oldies.
    I know someone who when he wakes up in the
Morning likes to just lie there and feel himself all over (maybe
    he's afraid he vanished in the night: I rather
Wish he would): I like to lie in bed at night and read and feel
    myself, shoulders, armpits, chest, belly, crotch,
And maybe tweak a hair. Once I found a kind of a swarm of moles
    on my rib cage—only I don't think they were
Moles: I don't know what they were, not scabies, not a rash: little
    lumps, growths, a colony. I put rubbing alcohol on
Them and in a few days they were gone. I don't like any funny
    business, stuff like that. Herpes simplex! That's a drag:
Eye salve is good for it, I found that out from a doc in Zurich
    where I stayed in a snow-white hotel beside the green glassy
And rushing river on which swans pointed upstream toward the
    bridge on whose balustrade I was drunkenly leaning one
January night when some men came by and spoke to me in
    German: "Surely you speak English?" I said: they thought
I was a gas. We went somewhere to drink and soon I was in bed
    with a supple, gray-haired man, playing snakes, flailing
About and knocking the bedside lamp on the floor. He ran one of
    the big hotels and used to send me packets of
Marrons glacés sprinkled with candied violets: the desk clerk
    gave me funny looks when he handed me
My daily tribute. How I gobbled them up! I wonder what my
    chum's name was? Once, when we were dining, the
String quartet played "Wien, Wien," and he leaned across the table
    and took my hand and said, "This will be our team
Song": it took a while to figure out what he meant. And once he
    said, "Come": we stepped into his bathroom,
He picked a razor up and shaved my sideburns off. What crust. I
    didn't really mind though: I'd only grown them
Because what else do you do on a nine-day crossing? What I did
    mind was that it emerged he was a major bore, so
I packed my duds and took an express train to Geneva, which I
    only went to because I wanted to stay at a hotel where

232

Henry James had stayed: it had fallen on sorry days and my view of
    Lake Leman was one of banks of fog. I walked past
Calvin's house on moist cobbles, bought a volume of Gide's diary,
    saw George Raft in *Scarface*, and took the train
To Italy, passing the inspiration of Byron's "The Prisoner of
    Chillon." Switzerland, so long. July is gone,
A hunk of August, a few blank days got lost (I couldn't stop
    sleeping), the sun came cloudlessly back, hot yesterday,
Hotter today, hotter still tomorrow the TV set predicts: shower
    baths help: I'm well bedewed this minute, my
Hair slicked down, and icy orange juice and iced tea with lemon—
    both are on my desk—no wonder my time is spent
Hanging out over the toilet, splashing away like a mountain
    rill. Late in the afternoon and suddenly a cool
Breeze springs up and streams in the window: the leaves shudder:
    how sweet, when something you really enjoy
Unexpectedly arrives, like the postcard I got this morning from
    Ned Rorem, with flattering words about some
Poems, how kind, how nice, but I'm glad I'm not with him on
    Nantucket, where I got one of the worst sunburns of my life—
I wonder what it's like, being a composer? Writing goes by so fast:
    a couple of hours of concentration, then you're
Spent: but music takes so much time: the sounds come into your
    head, but then, the writing them down, the little
Notes. I can see Nantucket now, sand and whipping grass under a
    glare of sun. There are not many islands I really
Like, the ones where the rocks are slithery under the
    thick seaweed when the tide is out, where the
Heart of the island beneath tall trees is all overgrown with ferns
    and moss begemmed with fog and is silent, spongy
To walk on: on other days, a scented springy mattress to stretch
    out on. Little boats emerge from behind other
Islands: utter peace and total privacy. Still, Nantucket has its
    points, but I prefer to go north and further north:
Maine, New Brunswick, Nova Scotia. Oh, what's to make such a
    fuss about? I like all sorts of places. I can't
Believe it, I have to go piss again: it's like that night in

Paris when I first got bombed on Pernod: I
Was making my way along the boulevard back to the hotel when
    my bladder flashed the message that I had to go and
I had to go *now*, not in two minutes: up ahead, in the same block,
    I could see a pissoir (I mean, a *vespasienne*)
But that just wasn't close enough, nor could I run. I plunged my
    left hand in my pocket, and got a good grip, like
Stopping the flow in a hose, and walked stiff-legged along: the
    pressure, the pain, was something else: "My
Brow was wet": I made it: there I was, confronting a urinal: I
    inched down my zipper and put my right hand into
The opening: hideous trauma, there was just no way I could
    transfer my swollen tool from hand to hand without a great
Gushing forth (inside my pants), like when Moses hit the rock: so
    I did it: there was piss all over Paris, not
To mention my shirt and pants, light sun tans: why couldn't it
    have been the depths of winter, and me in heavy
Dark overcoat? I was so mad I stomped on my way, thinking, "Well
    if somebody wants to make something out of it . . ."
(Young and dumb, it never occurred to me that if I'd spilled a
    drink in a café, I'd have looked the same.)
But Pernod, Pernod is murder. I wish I had some now, but tea
    and orange juice will have to do:
Tomorrow: New York: in blue, in green, in white, East Aurora
    goodbye.

FROM

A Few Days

[1 9 8 5]

A Few Days

For Tom Carey

are all we have. So count them as they pass. They pass
    too quickly
out of breath: don't dwell on the grave, which yawns for
    one and all.
Will you be buried in the yard? Sorry, it's against
    the law. You can only
lie in an authorized plot but you won't be there to
    know it so why worry
about it? Here I am at my brother's house in western
    New York: I came
here yesterday on the Empire State Express, eight hours
    of boredom on the train.
A pretty blond child sat next to me for a while. She
    had a winning smile,
but I couldn't talk to her, beyond "What happened to
    your shoes?" "I put them under the seat." And
so she had. She pressed the button that released the
    seat and sank
back like an old woman. Outside, purple loosestrife
    bloomed in swathes
that turned the railway ditch and fields into a
    sunset-reflecting lake.
And there was goldenrod and tattered Queen Anne's Lace
    and the noble Hudson
on which just one sailboat sailed, billowing, on a
    weekday afternoon.
A tug towed some scows. Sandy red earth and cows,
    the calves like
big dogs. With Fresca and ham and cheese on a roll,
    eight hours somehow passed.
My sister-in-law met me at the Buffalo Central Station
    and drove me out to their house.
Hilde is just back from a visit home to Augsburg,

237

where she was born

not too long ago. She taught herself to speak English, which
she does extremely well.

My mother now lives with them in the house my brother built.
She's old: almost eighty-nine

and her sight is failing. She has little to do but sit and
listen to the TV rumble.

When I came in she said, "I can't see you but I know your
voice!"

"Some corner of a garden where the soul sinks down under
its own weight . . ."

But this isn't about my family, although I wish it were. My
niece Peggy is at

camp in the Adirondacks so I am staying in her room.
It's essence of teen-age

girl: soft lilac walls, colored photographs of rock stars,
nosegays of artificial flowers,

signs on the door: THIS ROOM IS A DISASTER AREA, and
GARBAGEDUMP.

"Some ash can at the world's end . . ." But this is not
my family's story, nor

is it Molly's: the coon hound pleading silently for table
scraps. The temperature

last night dipped into the forties: a record for August
14th. There is a German

down pouff on the bed and I was glad to wriggle under
it and sleep the sleep

of the just. Today a perfection of blue: the leaves
go lisp in the breeze.

I wish I were a better traveler; I love new places, the
arrival in a station

after the ennui of a trip. On the train across the aisle
from me there was a young couple.

He read while she stroked the flank of his chest in a
circular motion, motherly,

covetous. They kissed. What is lovelier than young love?
Will it only lead

to barren years of a sour marriage? They were perfect
    together. I wish
them well. This coffee is cold. The eighteen-cup pot
    like most inventions
doesn't work so well. A few days: how to celebrate them?
    It's today I want
to memorialize but how can I? What is there to it?
    Cold coffee and
a ham-salad sandwich? A skinny peach tree holds no
    peaches. Molly howls
at the children who come to the door. What did they
    want? It's the wrong
time of year for Girl Scout cookies.
My mother can't find her hair net. She nurses a cup of
    coffee substitute, since
her religion (Christian Science) forbids the use
    of stimulants. On this
desk, a vase of dried blue flowers, a vase of artificial
    roses, a bottle with
a dog for stopper, a lamp, two plush lions that hug
    affectionately, a bright
red travel clock, a Remington Rand, my Olivetti, the
    ashtray and the coffee cup.
Moonlight Serenade:
        Moon, shine in my yard,
        let the grass blades
        cast shadows on themselves.
        Harbinger of dreams,
        let me sleep in your
        eternal glow.
That was last night. Today, the color of a buttercup,
    winds on the spool
of time, an opaque snapshot. Today is better than yesterday,
    which was too cold for
August. Still, it had its majesty of tumultuous cloud wrack.
    Here and there a sunbeam
struggled through. Like the picture in my grandmother's Bible

of Judgment Day:
Rembrandtesque beams of spotlights through cloud cities on a
   desolate landscape. I
used to feel frightened when I saw that effect in the sky. The
   August coolness:
a winter's-coming autumn feeling of it's time to pull our
   horns in and snuggle
down for winter. The radio, the anodyne of the lonely, speaks
   or rather sings:
                    I love you only
                    don't want to be lonely
delectable, deleterious trash. Three in the afternoon, when
   time stands still.
Is your watch right? Rest after labor doth greatly ease. There is
   no place to put
anything. These squandered minutes, hours, days. A few days, spend
   them riotously. There
is no occasion for riot. I haven't had a drink in years, begging
   a few glasses of
wine. I dream at night about liquor: I was mad at Fairfield because
   he invited people
to dinner and all he bought for them to drink was a pint of rum.
   I poured some for Anne
in a crumbling eggshell. And what does it mean? I'm no
   good at interpreting
dreams. Hands fumble with clothes, and just at the delirious
   moment I wake up:
Is a wet dream too much to ask for? Time for a cigarette. Why are
   pleasures bad for you?
But how good the tobacco smoke tastes. Uhm. Blow smoke rings
   if you can. Or
blow me: I could do with a little carnal relief. The yard slopes
   down to a swampy bit,
then fields rise up where cows are pastured. They do nothing
   all day but eat:
filling their faces so they'll have a cud to chew on. I'm not
   uncowlike myself: life as a

continuous snack. Another ham-salad sandwich and then goodbye.
    Will you say no to a
stack of waffles? I need a new pastime: photography turned out to
    be just too expensive. I
miss it though, stalking the motif, closing in on a flower, my
    photograph of Katherine Koch
laughing and leaning back in a porch that blazed with sunlight.
    Ei, you went off to Naropa
in Boulder, Colorado, and I have a postcard to prove it.
    I think about your
lesbian love for your roommate. You're a modern miss and I like
    you as you are.
Today is tomorrow, it's that dead time again: three in the afternoon
    under scumbled clouds,
livid, that censor the sun and withhold the rain: impotent as
    an old man ("an
old man's penis: limp as a rabbit's ear"). It's cool
    for August and I
can't nail the days down. They go by like escalators, each alike,
    each with its own
message of tears and laughter. I could go pick beans only Hilde
    beat me to it.
The drive to the village: a whole generation younger than I
    seem to rule the
roost. Where Sipprell the photographer used to live and work
    is someone else's
now. He was a kind and gentle man. I knew his sons. The one I
    knew best is dead
and gone now, as he is himself. Life sends us struggling forth
    like "the green vine
angering for life" and rewards us with a plate of popovers
    labeled "your death."
Where is mine waiting? What will it be like when there's no
    more tomorrow? I
can't quite escape the feeling of death as a sleep
    from which we awaken
refreshed, in eternity. But when the chips are down I plunk

them on nothingness;
my faith ran out years ago. It may come back, but I doubt it.
    "Rest in peace"
is all I have to say on the subject. I drink too much strong
    German coffee and
can't sleep at night. Last night I woke up laughing from
    a beautiful sensual
dream: a man who looked like a handsome woman who looked like
    a man. He told
me I should read in the sun to get a better color. But oh, the
    delicate touchings!
Venison stew, rank and gamey. Choke it down. Have a dumpling.
    Once again it's
another day, a gray day, damp as a dog's mouth, this unlikely
    August. In the vegetable
plot the squash are ripening, and tomatoes. Perhaps there are
    nematodes: cucumbers
won't grow here. They start to produce and then the plants die
    back. In the garden
(the flower garden) edelweiss thrives and so do China asters.
    Here, at home, I'm
lonelier than alone in my New York digs. There is no one to talk
    to, nothing to talk
about. "Tell me the story of your life," in great detail. Your first
    memory, the scariest thing
that ever happened: travels and food, the works. "Are you really
    interested?" "Passionately."
When you rest your head like that you suddenly look like an
    old woman, the old
woman you may one day become. Struggle into the shower to wash
    your hair, then crimp
it in rollers. You have a corrugated head. Can't you throw
    caution to the winds
and buy a little of some decent scent? Scent is one of the great
    amenities. Smelling like
a whore's dream. The dream shop and the dram shop. Dram shops
    in Amsterdam, old and cozy

242

enclosing the small fires of marvelous *ginevra*. It burns
   my throat and my eyes water;
so good to be free in the mid-afternoon, free to be a slightly
   drunk tourist, eyeing
the man-made wonders along the Amstel. Go to Naples to buy
   striped socks off a barrow.
Besides the dram shops there is the Pleasure Chest, with its
   edifying displays: pleasure takes
   many forms: keep it
simple is the best bet. I especially hate the picture of two
   Scotties with pink bows
on their heads. Sentimentality can go further than the door to
   the cellar and the
braid of garlic. Guess I'm ready for lunch: ready as I'll
   ever be, that is.
Lunch was good: now to move my bowels. That was good too:
   "Oh shit," she said,
"I stepped in some doggy pooh." Worse things could happen
   to you. Meeting a
man-eating tiger in the street, for instance. A little
   trembling worthless
thing: a mobile. It balances five angels and I lie in bed
   and throw puffs of
breath at it. It does its shimmering dance. Sunday, "the
   worst day," and we
all sit snowbound in drifts of Sunday paper. No news is
   good news but it
sure makes Jack a dull boy. "I can't get in there: my grades
   aren't good enough."
My nephew Mike came home at two in the morning from his
   hitchhiking trip in the Middle West. He
liked Springfield, Mo., the best. I can't make out why: a
   girl perhaps. He's
sixteen and smokes, which makes my brother see red. I wanted
   to ask him if he ever
smokes pot, but a sudden shyness came over me, the way
   the white sky overcame

this bluest of mornings. A sound of rolling peas:
    traffic goes by.
"Is Fred your uncle?" my mother asked out of the dimness
    of time. "No: he's
my kid brother." "Oh, I see." It's time for Hilde
    to brush and comb
her hair, a glory of white. She sits all day, a monument
    to patience, almost eighty-nine
if she's a day. We talk, but nothing comes of it. Minnesota
    winters when the sleighs
whirled over the snow-covered fences and jokes were
    made about the Scandinavians.
Exhilaration: one night we took the toboggan and went
    to Emery Park, where
there was a long, long slide, on which we sped
    into the night. "I'll
wash your face in the snow!" "Get away from me, you
    punk rock rabbit."
I just sat outside with my mother: my one good deed
    of the day.
That day passed like any other and I took the train from
    Buffalo to New York.
Buffalo, the city God forgot. Not even the Pope is going
    to visit it,
and he should: it's the largest Polish city in the world.
    Now I'm back
in New York on West 23rd Street with the buses farting
    past. And the one
dog that barks its head off at two or three in the morning.
    I hate to miss
the country fall. I think with longing of my years in
    Southampton, leaf-turning
trips to cool Vermont. Things should get better as you
    grow older, but that
is not the way. The way is inscrutable and hard to handle.
    Here it is
the Labor Day weekend and all my friends are out of town:

just me and some
millions of others, to whom I have not yet been introduced.
    A walk in the
streets is not the same as a walk on the beach, by
        preference, a beach
emptied by winter winds. A few days, and friends will
        trickle back to
town. Dinner parties, my favorite form of entertainment.
    Though in these
inflationary times you're lucky to get chicken in
        place of steak.
What I save on meals I spend on taxis. Lately a lot
        of cabs have
signs: NO SMOKING, PLEASE, or NO SMOKING DRIVER ALLERGIC.
    A quiet smoke in
a taxi is my idea of bliss. Yes, everything gets more
        restricted, less free.
Yet I am free, one of the lucky ones who does not
        have to show up
Monday morning at some boring desk. I remember the years
        at NBC, looking
discontentedly out at grimy Sixth Avenue, waiting for
        the time to pass.
It did. Pass, I mean, and I took ship for Europe. A
        pleasant interlude
on the whole, despite my operation. I miss Rino, my
        Roman lover, and
often wonder how he is and what he's up to. Probably
        a grandfather by
now. Good day, Signor Oscari: are you still a grocer
        by trade? Did
your uncle die and leave you his shop in the *periferia*?
        Italy seems so
far away (a few hours by plane), and, you see,
        since I was there
I fell in love with an island in Maine, now out of
        bounds. I'd like to

245

find a new place, somewhere where there are friends and
    not too many
houses. This summer has passed like a dream. On the last
    day of August
I feel much better than I felt in June, heaven be praised.
    Who said, "Only
health is beautiful"? There's truth in the old saw. I
    have always been
more interested in truth than in imagination: I
    wonder if that's
true? I have one secret, which I sometimes have an almost
    overwhelming desire
to blurt out; but I won't. Actually, I have told it to
    my shrink, so it's
not an absolute secret anymore. Too bad. Are secrets a
    way of telling lies,
I wonder? Yes, they are. So, let it be. I don't drink
    anymore, still, I
just had four double cocktails: margaritas. At least I
    stopped there. I
like not drinking. Hangovers were too horrible. I MEAN THAT.
    Really mean that.
Tomorrow is another day, but no better than today if
    you only realize it.
Let's love today, the what we have now, this day, not
    today or tomorrow or
yesterday, but this passing moment, that will
    not come again.
Now tomorrow is today, the day before Labor Day,
    1979. I want to
live to see the new century come in: but perhaps it's
    bad luck to
say so. To live to be seventy-six: is that so much
    to ask? My father
died in his forties, but his mother lived to be ninety,
    as my mother seems
likely to. In what rubbishy old folks' home will I

pass my sunset years?
A house on the edge of a small town, private but
    convenient, is my
wish. I won't say no to Vermont or Maine, not that
    I want to spend
my old age shoveling snow. I spent my youth doing
    that. Our drive
was cut into the side of a hill and no sooner
    was it cleared
than the wind would drift it full again. Monotonous
    days, daydreaming
of any place but there. It rained earlier today: I
    lay on the bed
and watched the beads it formed on the foliage of
    my balcony balustrade
drop of their own weight. I remember the night the
    house in Maine
was struck by lightning. It was attracted to a
    metal flue
and coursed harmlessly down to the wood-burning
    stove that heated
the bath water for my end of the house. I could
    write a book about
the island, but I don't want to. I want to write
more novels. I've made more false starts than anyone
    since Homer was a
pup. Now it's dinnertime: time to feed the inner man. I
    wish I could go
on a diet of water for a few days: to reduce the outer
    man to weigh what
he should weigh. A letter from Joe Brainard: he's
    my favorite pen pal.
Joe decides what he's going to do, then he does it.
    This summer it's
been sunbathing and reading Dickens and Henry James.
    And he sends a poem:
        "Ah! the good old days!"

"If gobbled then—digested now.
(Clarified by time—romanticized by mind.)
For today's repast remembered."
     and:
"Reminds me of you—Jimmy—out in
Southampton in the big Porter House in your
little room of many books it takes game-
board strategy to relocate now, as then."
     and:
"Out trekking up South Main Street
you are:
a pair of thick white legs
sporting Bermuda shorts
(of a *most* unusual length)
and plain blue sneakers so 'you'
they are."
I tripped and fell the other night and struck the curb
     with my head,
face forward. I went to the emergency at St. Vincent's.
     They put stitches
in my chin: I look like "The Masque of the Red Death."
     Feel like it, too.
I wish this humid unsunny day would get its act together
     and take it on the road.
It's no day for writing poems. Or for writing, period.
     So I didn't.
Write, that is. The bruises on my face have gone, just
     a thin scab on
the chin where they put the stitches. I'm back on Antabuse:
     what a drag. I
really love drinking, but once I'm sailing I can't seem
     to stop. So, pills
are once again the answer. It must have been horrible
     to live before
the days of modern medicine—all those great artists going
     off their chump
from syphilis or coughing their lungs out with TB. But

they still haven't
found a live-forever pill. But soon. Across the street
          sunlight falls like
a shadow on the Palladian office building. This room
          faces north, which
usually I don't like, but the French doors to the
          balcony make it light
enough. I ought to buy a plant, but plants are too much
          like pets: suppose
you want to go away (and I do), someone has to take care
          of it. So I waste my
money on cut flowers. I'm spoiled: I'm used to gathering
          flowers for the house,
not buying them. Thirty-five dollars for a dozen roses,
          Sterling Silver:
not today. Always thinking about what things cost: well,
          I have to, except
when a cab comes in my view: then I flag it down.
          I'd be scared to
figure up how much I spend a year on chauffeur-driven
          comfort. I'd like to spend
          part of this lovely
day in a darkened movie theater: only there's nothing I
          want to see. Fellini's
Orchestra Rehearsal was too much like *Alice in Orchestralia*.
          Perhaps a good
walk is more what's called for. I could tool down to
          Dave's Pot Belly
and have a butterscotch sundae: eating on the pounds I
          walked off. Or
I could go shopping: I need cologne. Taylor's Eau de Portugal
          for choice. In the
country you can take a walk without spending money. In
          the city it isn't
easy. This soft September sun makes the air fizzy like
          soda water: Perrier
in the odd-shaped bottle from France. I dreamed last

night about autumn
trees: orange, red, yellow, and the oaks dark green. I
    wish there were
something besides ginkgos and plane trees to see short
    of Central Park.
"It does wonders for your back . . ." The radio is on:
    perhaps this will
be a lucky day and they'll play something besides the
    New World Symphony
or Telemann. I could call Ruth and chat, only it isn't
    noon so she
isn't up yet. It still isn't noon: it's tomorrow
    morning. The risen
sun almost comes in the north windows: I see it lie
    along the balcony,
cut into shapes by the wrought-iron balustrade, a
    design of crazy
chrysanthemums and willow leaves. This old hotel is
    well built: if
you hold your breath and make a wish you'll meet Virgil
    Thomson in the elevator
or a member of a punk rock band. I still want to go to
    a movie but
there isn't any. A month ago when I wasn't in the
    mood there were lots:
Flying Down to Rio, Million Dollar Legs, Blonde Bombshell
    or do I date myself?
A red, pink and blue slip on my desk tells me that
    I am going to
spend forty dollars to have a jacket relined. A child
    of the thirties,
that seems to me what you spend for a new suit. More
    money! I got that
cologne: sixteen-twenty. Think I'll splash some on
    right now. Uhm. Feels good.
    And take a shower.
No. That would mean taking my clothes off and putting

250

them on again. I

haven't got the energy for that. And the waste of hot water!
And I should wash my hair.

But that would mean putting my shoes on and a tromp around
the corner to the

drugstore that isn't open yet. Or I could wash it with plain
cucumber soap and

rinse it with lime juice (I think there is a lime). I
think I'll leave it matted

and get it cut—oh—tomorrow. For a while I let it get
really long, I

looked like Buffalo Bill's mother. Ruth says, "Oh, Jimmy,
you look much better

with short hair." "Graciousness, part of the Japanese
character." The radio

is still on. "It's time for one of our classical hits:
you'll recognize this

one." But I don't. Good grief, it's "Greensleeves." I'm
a real music lover!

I'd rather listen to rock, but if I tune WNCN out I
can never find it

again. Last night they played the Brahms Second Piano
Concerto, which sent

me off contentedly to bye-bye land. The sleeping pills
I scoffed helped too.

It used to be when I checked out a medicine chest there
would be lots of

amphetamines. No more. Doctors won't prescribe them.
I heard a rumor

about a diet doctor in Queens who will. Must find out
his address. But

Queens seems awfully far to give the day a gentle lift.
I can do it with

coffee, only that much coffee gives me sour stomach. Urp.
Belch. Guess I'll

make a cup of Taster's Choice. My sister-in-law and
Donald Droll both use

that brand. Not bad. *The Burning Mystery of Anna in 1951:*
    I prefer the genteel wackiness
of John Ashbery's *As We Know.* A poem written in two
    columns, supposed to
be read simultaneously: John is devoted to the impossible.
    The sunlight still
sits on my balcony, invitingly. I decline the invitation:
    out there, it gives
me vertigo. People who come here say, "Oooh, you have a
    balcony," as though I
spent my days out there surveying 23rd Street:
    Chelsea Sewing Center,
Carla Hair Salon. 23rd Street hasn't got much
    going for it, unless
you love the YMCA. I once did. I remember Christmas '41.
    I was in the shower
when a hunk walked in. I got a hard-on just like that.
    He dropped his soap
to get a view of it and in no time we were in bed in
    his room. Sure was
a change from West Virginia. When I told Alex Katz I
    went to college in West
Virginia, he said in that way of his, "Nah,
    you're Harvard." Wish I
were, but I'm a lot more panhandle than I am Cambridge,
    Mass. Which reminds
me, I saw in the *Times* that my old friend Professor Billy
    Vinson died of the
heart condition he knew he had. Billy was the Navy officer
    who, when he was
getting fucked by an apelike sailor, lifted his head out of
    the pillow and
said, "I order you back to your ship." His camp name was
    Miss Williemae.
He was a virologist who detected two new viruses, which he
    named for Chester
Kallman and me: Fiordiligi and Dorabella. If anybody called

me by my camp name
nowadays I'd sock them—I like to think. I remember how
    I felt when Chester
dedicated his book to me and wrote the poem in "camp": "Wearing
    a garden hat her mother
wore . . ." Bitch. Chester's gone now, and so are Wystan, Billy
    Vinson, Brian Howard, Bill Aalto and Brian's
friend, the red-haired boy whose name I can't remember.
    Chester was a martyr
to the dry martini. So, in his way, was Wystan. Brian
    committed suicide:
Why do people do that? For fun? Brian was the most
    bored and boring man
I ever met. He was what the French call *épatant*: he told
    an American officer
that he was a clandestine homosexual. The officer knocked
    him to the barroom floor.
Brian looked up and said, "That proves it." I could tell
    a thousand Brian
stories, the way some people can reel off limericks. For
    a great poet, Wystan
Auden's dirty limericks are singularly uninspired. Sorry
    I can't remember any
to quote you. *The Platonic Blow* gives me hives. Funny porn
    I guess is a gift,
like any other. Who wrote:
    Lil tried shunts and double-shunts
    And all tricks known to common cunts . . .?
A tired newspaperman? A gifted coal miner in West
    Virginia? The morning
passes like an elephant in no stampede. The morning passes like
    Salome's veil. Last
lines: "I am still alive!" and "Kill that woman!" Fast
    curtain. The morning
passes too slowly. I want it to be seven-forty-five in the evening,
    when I'm invited
to dine on delectables *chez* John Ashbery. I wonder if the

253

cuisine will be
Indian? The little minx took a course in it, after all
    those years in France.
Tall Doug and blond Frank will be there: I wonder about
    David Kermani of the
shoe-button eyes? Lately whenever I've gone there he's
    been out on some
important errand: is he avoiding me? I hope not. I like
    him. What a
devil he is for work. I hope his boss, Tibor, values him
    at his true worth.
The sun is off the balcony. The sun is off: a scrim of
    cloud obscures the
sky. Yesterday was such a heaven day: blue, warm, breezy.
    When I cabbed up to Barbara's
I found the park full of joggers: men and women whose
    breasts and buttocks
went jounce, jounce. Uhm: a shave and a splash of Eau
    de Portugal,
Taylor's best. I mustn't use it up too fast: think what
    it cost. The only trouble
with it is that it doesn't hang on: I like a cologne that
    makes people say, "You
smell good," like Guerlain's Impériale. Paco
    really hangs on:
people who say "You smell so good" look as though
    they're going to retch.
I threw caution to the winds and threw it out. I
    would like to go
in the bathroom and swizzle on some of Taylor's best,
    but the maid is in
there stinking up the house with household ammonia.
    "Is that girl who
comes and takes care of you your niece?" she asked me.
    No, Eileen Myles is
my assistant: she comes and makes my breakfast and
    lunch, runs errands

to the grocery store, the P.O., the bank, mails letters,
    and always arrives with
that morning's *Times*. I lie in bed and read the obituaries
    and smell the French
toast frying. Served with applesass. I think I'll
    let her take the laundry
out; she needs the exercise. The sun is off the balcony,
    the air is cool
as one of Barbara's kisses, which don't make me feel
    I turn her on.
Her husband won't give her money to pay the cleaning
    woman and they
have a huge co-op. It is all neat and tidy. Barbara is
    very organized
for a literary lady. She loaned me a book about Natalie
    Barney I thought
would be fascinating but the writing is much too coy,
    "Amazon" instead of
dyke or Lesbian. I always think I can read anything
    but some things turn me off:
like trying to read jellied gasoline. I could almost
    put a sweater on
the air from the French doors is so cool. But I think
    I like to live
cold, like George Montgomery and Frank O'Hara wearing
    chinos and sneakers
in the snow at Harvard. It was the thing to do. "I'd like
    to kiss Jimmy," said
a dope who came to the door. Frank made a grand gesture at
    me lying reading on
the couch and said, "Help yourself." So he did. I wonder
    what I was reading?
I should keep a reading diary of all the books and mags
    I read, but what
would be the use? I can't remember what I read. I read
    Graham Greene's A
Sort of Life and a week later reread it without remembering

anything, except his
playing Russian roulette. It's a lovely book, the writing
    is so concrete. I
have a foible for books of family life, like Gwen Raverat's
    Period Piece and
Frances Marshall's A *Pacifist's War*. I went out to post
    some letters (Chemical
Bank, Denver Art Museum, my lawyer) and
    the sun was hot. In
the shadows it was cool but when you stepped into a sun-
    spot you felt the heat.
It's a beautiful day, the gray nimbus devoured itself. No
    clouds at all.
I bought the *Post*. More mothers killing their babies be-
    cause they're mad
at their husbands. What kind of sense does that make? Maybe
    they wanted to have
abortions and their husbands wouldn't let them. How
    does that grab you?
Eileen took the double-breasted blazer Joe Hazan
    gave me to have
the sleeves shortened half an inch. It came from Hunts-
    man! I used to have a
Huntsman hacking raincoat. In Alex Katz's painting
    Incident you can see
me wearing it, flanked by Ada Katz in a hat and Rudi
    Burckhardt with a
camera. That was a long time ago. I wonder if they still
    have their Teddy Wilson
record? The Alicia de Larrocha of the hot piano.
    A few days! I
started this poem in August and here it is September
    19th. September
is almost my favorite month, barring October and May.
    November, my natal
month, is too damn wintry, I don't like it but I like
    my birthstone, the topaz.

256

In Venice I saw a pair of cufflinks, square topazes
        edged with paste
diamonds—sixty-five bucks, but Arthur, who was
        picking up the check,
wouldn't buy them for me. Cheap is cheap. It was funny
        having no money of
my own. Every time I went out sightseeing I would see
        a black-and-red knitted
tie I wanted passionately to own. Last weekend I spent
        at Barbara's in
Water Mill: a funny turreted house, commodious within
        (this coffee is too strong),
all the woodwork very 1900, dark wood balusters
        and cream walls,
Barbara's pictures: Paul Georges, Robert Goodenough, Fairfield
        Porter. We went
to call on Anne Porter, who is selling the house at 49 South
        Main, where I used
to live. The library was void of books: it made me sad, the
        way it did when
my mother sold her house. That one back room in the ell was
        my room. I could
lie in the four-poster on the horsehair mattress and stare
        at Fairfield's color
lithograph of Sixth Avenue and the Waverly Theater en-
        tranced by its magic.
The cover of *Hymn to Life* is Fairfield's version of the
        view from my
south window: the wondrous pear tree in white bloom. Did
        you know that you
can force pears to bloom? Go out in the snow and cut a
        few knobbly twigs
with buds. Soak them overnight in water, put them in a vase
        and hold your breath:
a Chinese print is what you have. A haircut: Breck's
        Shampoo for Normal Hair.
I looked for *The New York Review of Books*, which has a

review in it of my novel
by Stephen Spender. Couldn't find it. Damn. It's funny,
    having a review come
out a whole year later. Everyone on the street was wearing
    sweaters. There was a
man lying on the sidewalk, one shoe off, his shirt un-
    buttoned down to his
navel. Passersby looked at him coldly; nobody offered
    to help him. I
curbed my Good Samaritan instincts. Poor guy: once he was
    a little boy. How
do you degenerate that way? There aren't any novels about
    blindstiffs these
days: *Tramping on Life* and Jim Tully. Joe Hazan, who lives
    in a Fifth Avenue penthouse,
went on the bum when he was young. I'm thinking about D.D.
    Ryan and her "mothwing" eyebrows.
She says they grew that way, but in a bright light I
    wondered.
She never appears until her face is on. Her boys, Beau and Drew,
    are match-happy. I went
outside and there in the autumn leaves was a circle of flame.
    We managed to stamp
it out. It was right by the house: Kenward's little cottage
    reduced to ashes! Almost.
D.D.'s Vuitton cosmetic trunk that weighed a ton. When we
    stopped at the diner
in Rutland I saw a stark-naked man in the john. He dashed
    into a stall and hid
himself. "I really hate to do this," D.D. said, passing a
    car on the right
at ninety miles an hour. "*On ne voit pas le rivage de la
    mort deux fois, D.D.,*"
as Racine said. When we got to New York Kenward and I
    went to Casey's and got hysterical with laughter.
Blossoming afternoon, what can I tell you? You tell me that
    my hair is clean and cut.

Breck's Shampoo for Normal Hair, 40¢ off. It's nice and
    gloopy. I'd like to
take a bubble bath but I haven't got the stuff. Bath oil
    is risky business:
it coats the tub with slime and taking a shower is a perilous
    stunt. Help! my Eau
de Portugal is half empty. I've been slathering it on. I
    love it. I ought to
get a Caswell-Massey sampler and see what smells best. Patchouli.
    Vetiver (ugh). September
evening, what have you to say to me? Tell me the time. Still
    two and three-quarter hours
until John's. I'm reading Osbert Sitwell's autobiography
    stitched in brocade. I
read a page, then rush back to my poem. I would once have
    thought that Sitwell
was "influencing" me. I'm too me for that. Poor trembling
    Osbert, suffering from
Parkinson's disease. I met him at a party Wystan gave for
    them. John was
dashing tears from his eyes: "What's wrong?" "I just met
    Edith Sitwell." Tender
heart. Edith looked less like her photographs. She was
    creased and had that
famous nose. September day, how shall I color you? In blue
    and white and airy tones.
September evening, you give your benediction. Ruth is
    in love with a priest
(an Episcopalian) who smokes grass. Ruth can convert from
    Judaism and wear a
hat in church. "The Overture to *Zampa* led by Leonard Bernstein
    with the New York
Philharmonic." The radio is such a pleasure. A Hand in
    a Glove: a vase
you couldn't believe. "Price includes round-trip air fare."
    Oh, the radio! I
can't live without it. Yes, I must put a sweater on. Brrr.

September, how fickle you are,
there is the shadow of a flapping flag. The Plaza Hotel
    was flying a Japanese
flag: who was staying there? I have on a George Schneeman
    T-shirt, a plaid
shirt on a coat hanger. Useless gas. Here is my Blue Cross/
    Blue Shield number: 11223677
H08. I don't know my social security number. It's in two
    names: James Ridenour
and James Schuyler. Ridenour was my stepfather's name,
    and when I went to
Europe in 1947 I found my name had never legally been
    changed. Sometimes someone
comes up to me and says, "Aren't you Jimmy Ridenour?" I
    plotz. It's good to
have your own name. Ask me, I'll tell you. It's pink!
    the light I mean
shining from the west on the office building. The sunset.
    That's the trouble with
a north view: you can't see the sunset. North is kinda dreary.
    Will it be dark
when I set out for John Ashbery's? It spooks me. His
    apartment is so nice:
full of French antiques and Oriental rugs and collectibles.
    An angel wing begonia
and wandering Jew, peperomia. He has willowware china
    which reminds me of
the Willow tea room, where I used to eat in eighth grade.
    Salisbury steak. Chop suey.
There were motifs from the willowware painted on the walls.
    It's Wednesday morning, but
later than I got up yesterday: the sun is off the balcony.
    There's a chill in the air,
I put on a Jaeger sweater, sand color. The dinner was
    nice: cold soup, veal
collops with a brown sauce, broccoli, noodles, pineapple
    upside-down cake, whipped cream.

The latter had rum in it and I ate it rather nervously but
     it didn't activate the Antabuse.
Rather nervously describes the way I was all evening: just
     sat and drank Perrier
and smoked. Didn't say a word, even when someone spoke to
     me. I meant to say
to John, "Is there any coffee in the house?" Instead I said,
     "Is there any liquor in
the house?" He looked astounded. I faced it out, didn't tell
     him what I really
meant. I have a sleeping-pill hangover; my head feels like
     Venetian glass. I
only took two pills, not three, which puts me to sleep but
     makes me feel crappy.
The *Times* says there's a vogue for pumps: Eileen and I did
     the galleries and I
watched the women's feet: they were all wearing sandals,
     very chic, especially
a black chick who had on a stylish suit. I thought I could
     beat the starting gun
by taking my pills at seven: seven Sleepeze, two Nembutal,
     the scoffed pills, three
antidepressant pills, a red pill that controls the side
     effects of the antidepressants.
I went to sleep like a babe, and here I am wide awake at
     eleven. Anne Dunn is here.
She can't see me until Saturday lunch. I wanted to have
     dinner with her tonight.
Christ, I feel shitty. I took two more sleeping pills and
     what I feel like. Creamed
shit. I lay in bed for an hour; it was torture. It's the
     witching hour of night.
I feel great. This is the morning; it's wonderful. I can't
     tell you about it.
It's a grand day. I feel cold and I
     mailed letters today:
Denver Art Museum, Chemical Bank (that should bring in

money), Savitsky, my lawyer: he pays my bills, like
the rent ($550). I went back to bed and slept some after
all. Eleven hours all told. Not bad
but I still have the old sleeping-pill hangover. "He brought
it on himself."
I know I'm going to regret it but still I do it—take that
one extra pill at
the wrong time. I could kick myself around the block. It's
getting light out
not sunlight, just morning gray. It looks the way it feels—
chill. THE LAW FIRM
OF RICHARD D. SAVITSKY, a card says. I wonder if I trust him?
There's no reason why
I shouldn't. I wonder how they broke the news to him. "There's
this guy who keeps
having nervous breakdowns and he can't pay the hospital
bills—state hospitals being of course out of the
question." Bellevue is proof of that: the scary patients,
the nothing to do, the
insolent staff (that one nice girl), the egg for breakfast,
One morning I had a bowl of Cream of Wheat, the black guy
sitting next to me said, "Hunh, putting sugar on
grits," so this is
what grits are, people stealing cigarettes out of your pajama
pocket while you sleep,
patients who will share a cigarette with you, you have to
be an enforced abstainer
to know you'll never give up smoking, Christ I'm cold,
the up-in-the-air TV you can't see, just a blur, the ennui,
the doctor: "If there's any more
smoking on this side smoking privileges will be taken away,"
that's when you know
you'll never give up smoking. When I was in you could
only smoke if you had money to buy the cigarettes.
I didn't have any money and had to depend on the charity of
others. It was surprising
how many there were who were charitable. I swore I'd never

262

give up smoking. I
did though. It turned me into a fiend. I took up the costly
    cigar. My first cigarette
tasted good. I talk big: I have a pain in my chest and
    worry about lung cancer.
Better make an appointment with the doc. I don't like my
    doctors, except the dentist and my shrink. "Come on
in, Jim." "What are you thinking about?" "Nothing." Not
    true: you're always thinking something.
I'm thinking about this poem. How to make it good, really
    good. I'm proud of my poems.
I wrote a poem about Ruth Kligman in which
    every line began "Ruth"—
talk about maddening. Ruth claimed to like it. When I
    told her it was a
stinker she said, "I didn't think it was one of your best."
    I've got to find that
notebook and tear it up, when I'm dead some creep will
    publish it in a thin
volume called *Uncollected Verse*. It will be a collector's
    item. I hate to think
of the contents of that volume. "Dorabella's Hat," "They
    Two Are Drifting Uptown on a
Bus." Bill Berkson asked me to send him any writings I had
    so I sent him "They Two." He didn't publish it. It's
very funny. The two are Frank and Larry. It's not a poem.
    It's a playlet. I used
to write lots of playlets. "Presenting Jane" is lost.
    It was produced. By
Herbert Machiz. It was horrible thanks to Herbert. When
    I first met Herbert
he said, "A nice-looking boy like you shouldn't have
    dirty fingernails." I blanched. I looked at my
nails: I felt creepy. "I work in a bookstore," I
    extenuated. "Is it
a secondhand bookstore?" he demanded. "No,
    it specializes in

263

English books." "English dirt." I recounted this to Frank,
      who broke out laughing!
"Jimmy, Herbert is a wit." Herbert dropped dead, on a
      rug? John Latouche
fell down a flight of stairs in a small gray clapboard cottage
      at Apple Hill
among the leaves at Calais (pronounced callous), Vermont.
      Wystan died in his sleep
in a hotel in ring-streeted Vienna not far from his
      country home in verdant
southern Austria: Austria utterly turns me off: the
      goldenesdachtel at Innsbruck
is the worst thing, except for the dragon of Klagenfurt,
      Egg-am-Fackersee. The train
through torrent-torn needle-clad (I mean trees like
      spruce, pines and firs)
mountains and granite-boulders, then you're in Italy
      among the lemon
lamps and *"Permesso,"* which means "Move or I will mow you
      down with this dolly of
bricks." Then there's *"Ti da fastidio?"* which means "If
      I smoke will it give you the fastids?"
Then one day
the telephone:
it's Hilde:
"Mother passed on
in her sleep
last night. No,
you needn't
come, it's not that
kind of a ceremony.
Fred is seeing
to it all right
now. The last
three months were
pretty grim."
And so I won't be

264

there to see my Maney
enearthed beside
my stepfather:
once when I was
home a while ago
I said I realized
that in his way he
loved me. "He did
not," my mother said.
"Burton hated you."
The old truth-teller!
She was so proud
in her last dim
years (ninety years
are still
a few days) to be
longest-lived of
the Slaters: for-
getting her mother
was the Slater, she
a Connor:
Margaret Daisy Connor Schuyler Ridenour,
rest well,
the weary journey done.

The Snowdrop

The sheath pierces the turf
and the flower unfurls: drooping,
pendent, white, three-petaled,
the corolla with a frill
of green: the virgin of the spring!
In earliest spring! (Reginald
Farrer hated snowdrops: in his
Yorkshire rock garden the rain
beat them down into the mud
and they got all dirty. Why not
pick a few, wash them off and
make a nosegay in a wineglass,
Reginald?) And when the flower
fades and dies, the stem
measures its length along the sod,
the seed pod swelling like
a pale green testicle.

This Notebook

is small and stamped,
MADE IN ITALY.
It's bound in
Florentine art paper:
a design in blue and brown
of Maltese crosses
and what looks like
bladder wrack. How it takes
me back! To our
pensione on Piazza Frescobaldi,
Ponte Santa Trinità
(replaced, in postwar '40s,
by a Bailey bridge),
the Via Tornabuoni, and
Doney's and Leland's, in
one of which
Ronald Firbank
dangled grapes—before
my time. When
I walked in Florence I
used to see it not
as the Medicis' stamping ground
but through the eyes
of one of Henry James's
heroes or heroines:
Isabel Archer, perhaps.
To walk up to
Bellosguardo, to look
and wonder and remember
what I never knew!
Little notebook, I
love you, and the friend
who gave me you.

Velvet Roses

Katie is making
velvet roses: next
to a green pair, she
fastens a bunch of
wooden spoons. How
striking they will
look, on the bodice
of her dance frock!

And Anne is cooking,
and Lizzie is there . . .

Sleeping again,
dreaming again

At Darragh's I

lie in bed and watch the night
rise slowly, implacably, out of
evening, darkening
the lance-shaped leaves of that
nut tree whose name I never
can remember: only, those leaves
are too wide to be called
lanceolate: why, they're oval!
(A childhood memory, the
cookies that were called "fruited
ovals," molasses with a
white icing, that came from the
grocer, not made at home, and
oval
oval
oval.) When a firefly dances
into my view (a black window):
another childhood memory:
in Maryland we used to catch
them and put them in jars
and watch their silent, sexy
signal. We also used to tear
their phosphor off: children
can be real fun people!

Or I sit on the porch as
a light rain slants down
onto the pond Darragh made,
the wind riffling the water
and the rain making rain rings
on it. Oriane, the lurcher,
wants in, wants out, full
of the *va et vient* of life
(speaking of French, did

you know that in Paris bi-
sexuality is known as
voile et vapeur? I
like that).

Then we all pile into
the Toyota and drive off
into the
World of Roses.

Amy Lowell Thoughts

What are you, banded one?

H.D.

The sea opened its lips
blue with cold
and coughed up
a cabin cruiser

Covertly, in the mist,
the sun
is fingering some spruce

Draped one,
speak.
Are you a larch?

Just at the surface
toothed rocks
spit foamy mouthwash

The Five Sisters birch clump
chopped down.
Thoughts
of Charlotte Mew.

Over the sea
she strolls
in fog shoes

Beaded Balustrade

The balustrade along my balcony
is wrought iron in shapes of
flowers: chrysanthemums, perhaps,
whorly blooms and leaves and
along the top a row of what look
like croquet hoops topped by a
rod, and from the hoops depend
water drops, crystal, quivering.
Why, it must be raining, in Chelsea,
NYC! How I wish I could look out
and see rain-washed grass, and is
it not forsythia time? There, where
I dream of, the elms are gone (Dutch
elm blight), but the giant plane
tree, last to leaf out, last to
shed (but that's not until almost
winter, half a year away, or
so), and the shrub roses, waiting
to do their stuff! Oh well, if
I haven't got that, at least I've
got a beaded balustrade . . .

People who see bubbles rise

For Darragh Park

may be swimming, not drowning,
or merely diving, rising.
Or watching goldfish in a tank.
Or, "That's a vodka and soda?"
"Yes, please."

I'm on a train (Bridgehampton–New York)
Darragh is with me, reading Proust
—in French, of course: India paper,
a brown leather binding, brown
as the October leaves we pass:
scrub oak, I guess. No, they
still are green. Leathery, but green.

This noon, or early afternoon, I
walked down through still-unharvested potatoes
(one chicory was in blue, blue bloom)
to Sag Pond—Sagaponack Pond, I mean.
Across it winter rye made its
incredible green haze, so soft, so clear,
and trees around a yellow house,
trees I didn't recognize, were
a deep wine red. To their right, maples
did their flamboyant thing.

The dogs, the chat, the dinners,
the insomnia and the sleep:
the lousy book about V. Sackville-West:
for me, a rather mixed-up weekend.
And yet I loved it. I always
love the garden and the house Bob made
and the way the early light comes

in the guest-room windows
through violet curtains. To lie there,
watching it, like someone diving,
who, open-eyed, sees bubbles rise.

En Route to Southampton

In a corner of a parlor-car
window, a thin crescent is
the moon. Below,
the sky on the horizon
is oily bilge.
The leafless trees go by,
the ugly houses,
the parlor car
is much too hot.
The whistle blows
its warning:
such very ugly houses.
But in that corner
of the window,
the ice-white,
eternal promise
of a new moon.

Fauré's Second Piano Quartet

On a day like this the rain comes
down in fat and random drops among
the ailanthus leaves—"the tree
of Heaven"—the leaves that on moon-
lit nights shimmer black and blade-
shaped at this third-floor window.
And there are bunches of small green
knobs, buds, crowded together. The
rapid music fills in the spaces of
the leaves. And the piano comes in,
like an extra heartbeat, dangerous
and lovely. Slower now, less like
the leaves, more like the rain which
almost isn't rain, more like thawed-
out hail. All this beauty in the
mess of this small apartment on
West 20th in Chelsea, New York.
Slowly the notes pour out, slowly,
more slowly still, fat rain falls.

Red Brick and Brown Stone

For Darragh Park

He arises. Oriane
the lurcher wants
her walk. Out into
the freeze. Oriane
pees and shits. The
shit is scooped up
in a doggy bag, ac-
cording to law ($100
fine) and is disposed
of somewhere.
The sun peers down
and sees them. Ov-
altine, a fag, WNCN:
unspeakable Telemann.
The dinner table is
mahogany: the silver
gleams. A carriage
clock chimes eight,
sweetly. The front
room north-facing
studio, its two long
windows divided by
a pier glass. Canvas,
eight by six, cars
charge down Ninth
Avenue straight at
you. Parked, a yellow
cab. A bending tree.
London Terrace, an
eighteenth-century
house now a shop,
work in progress.
Brush in pigment:

scrub stroke scour.
Hours pass. Hunger
strikes: Empire Diner
silver metal art deco.
A porkburger, salad,
tea (iced). Home. Oriane
wants out. So they do
as before. Oriane goes
home. Off by cab to
Florentine palazzo
Racquet Club: naked,
the pool, plunge, how
many laps? Home. (Through-
out the day, numerous
cigarettes. I forget
which brand. Tareytons.)
A pencil drawing of
a vase of parrot tulips.
Records: Richter:
Scriabin: Tosca: "Mario!
Mario! Mario!" "I
lived for art, I
lived for love." Sup-
per: a can of baked
beans, a cup of raspberry
yoghurt. Perrier. Out?
A flick? An AA
meeting? Walk Oriane.
Nine p.m. Bed. A
book, V. Woolf's let-
ters. Lights out, sleep
not quite right away.
No Valium. The night
passes in black chiffon.

What Ails My Fern?

My peonies have lovely leaves
but rarely flower.
Oh, they have buds
and plenty of them. These
grow to the size of peas
and stay
that way.
Is this
bud blast?

What ails my fern?

I enclose a sample
of a white disease
on a leaf
of honesty
known also
as the money plant

My two blue spruce
look worse and worse

What ails my fern?

Two years ago a tenant
wound tape around my tree.
Sap dripped out of the branches
on babies in buggies below. So
I unwound the tape.
Can nothing be done
to revive my tree?

What ails my fern?

I hate my disordered
back-yard fence
where lilac, weigela
and mock orange grow.
Please advise
how to get rid of it.

Weeping willow roots
reaching out
seeking water
fill my cesspool and well.
What do you suggest?

What ails my fern?

Procession

Serene and purple twilight of the South
the wind-distorted olives
so dim beside the road
so very still tonight
the sea delicately touches
the shore with foam

Black clad, glimmer of white
pyramids of trembling gold
up the white road wind
in misty iris blue

a cross, a crown, a spear

the air is drenched

the nails, the hammer

fragrance of lemon and orange

the scourge, a sponge

salt perfume of the sea

Tom

They told me, Heraclitus, they told me you were dead.

A key. The door. Open
shut. "Hi, Jim." "Hi,
Tom." "How didja sleep?"
"I didn't. And you?" "A
log." Blond glory, streaked,
finger-combed, curling
in kiss curls at the nape.
A kiss, like bumping fore-
heads. A god, archaic Greek
Apollo in a blue down
jacket. Fifteen degrees
no snow. Tom hates that;
me too. "French toast?"
"Of course." With apple-
sauce. The *Times*, the
obits, a great blues singer
has been taken from us
and a businessman. OJ,
coffee with milk, lecithin
to control mouth movements,
a side effect of Thorazine.
At the stove Tom sings the
release of his rock song,
"Manhattan Movie." His voice
is rich, true, his diction
perfect. I'm so in love
I want to die and take
my happiness to heaven!
No. To be with Tom
three hours
a day four days a week.
(Tom likes "assistant"
I

prefer "secretary."
No sweat: "Ain't no
flies on the lamb
of God." Ahem. Phlegm.)
Tom's eyes are "twin
compendious blue oceans in
which white sails and
gulls wildly fly." We'll
never make it. Tom's
twenty-eight, I'm fifty-
six: he isn't Proust's
"young man born to love
elderly men." He loves E.,
an eighteen-year-old
poet, whose mother feels
concern at Tom's two-
year pursuit (they only
lately made it). I'm
going to tell her how
lucky her son is, if he
is to have a homosexual
episode (or be one, as
I think he is, pretty
boy), to have a lover so
kind, so loving, so
witty—that thrash-about
laugh—I've said it
and I will. At Number
One Fifth Avenue I tell
E., "You should un-
reservedly make love
to Tom and be cosy and
tender." "I'm sorry, I
don't feel that way
about him." Later
he tells Tom,
"We had a man-

to-man talk." Sad.
I care only about Tom's
happiness. "He's not
very sexually oriented.
Here." The French toast
and applesauce are
delicious. We settle down
to read: he, a Ross
Macdonald, me *Phineas
Redux*. How superb is
Mme Goesler when she
repudiates the Duke of
Omnium's bequest of
pearls and diamonds and
a fortune (she already
has one) so they will
go to Lady Glencora, the
rightful heir, and no one
can ever say her three years'
tenderness to the dying
man was motivated. In
Tom's book a corpse is
found in corrupt upper-
middle-class L.A., where
he comes from. Beauty.
We might some
day shower
together, wash
each other's back.
Traveling share a bed.
Flesh on flesh,
a head pillowed
on an arm. Touch.
Running from a cab to
the deli, the energy
(grace) of youth.
Thomas Paul Carey of

Sherman Oaks, California,
who writes and sings
his own rock songs, the
son and grandson of two
great movie actors, the
two Harry Careys. Love
is only and always beautiful.

Suddenly

it's night and Tom
comes in and says,
"It's pouring buckets
out," his blond hair
diamond-dusted with
raindrop fragments.

Index of Titles